Light Footprint Management

Light Footprint Management

Leadership in times of change

Charles-Edouard Bouée

Bloomsbury Information
An imprint of Bloomsbury Publishing Plc

B L O O M S B U R Y

LONDON · NEW DELHI · NEW YORK · SYDNEY

Bloomsbury Information

An imprint of Bloomsbury Publishing Plc

50 Bedford Square	1385 Broadway
London	New York
WC1B 3DP	NY 10018
UK	USA

www.bloomsbury.com

BLOOMSBURY and the Diana logo are trademarks of Bloomsbury Publishing Plc

First published in 2000 by A&C Black Business Information and Development
Reprinted by Bloomsbury Information 2014

British Library Cataloguing-in-Publication Data
A catalogue record for this book is available from the British Library.

HB: 978-1-4729-0005-0
PB: 978-1-4729-0385-3

Library of Congress Cataloging-in-Publication Data
A catalog record for this book is available from the Library of Congress

Design by Fiona Pike, Pike Design, Winchester
Typeset by Hewer Text UK Ltd, Edinburgh

This book is dedicated to my beloved wife Valérie
and to my two darling daughters,
Laure-Victoire and Charlotte-Alicia.

Contents

Acknowledgements   ix

Preface   xi

Introduction   1

1 Unfit for purpose   5

2 Presages   29

3 A new environment   45

4 A child of VUCA   61

5 Light footprint   77

6 Four characteristics   97

7 The LFP organization   119

8 Managing the LFP organization   135

9 Enlightened leadership   157

10 Building an LFP organization   173

Index   191

Acknowledgements

This book is a distillation and synthesis of my own experiences as a consultant working for two decades in over 20 countries, and the ideas, curiosity and bafflement of many other people: colleagues, clients, friends and chance acquaintances in Asia, Europe and the US, some of whom I met and talked with at my own crossroads in the sky, the Shanghai–Paris shuttle.

My thanks to all of them, particularly to Laurent Chouraki and Olivier Le Grand, for sharing their insights and running real-life, large-scale experiments with me. I hope that this book does justice to their observations and goes some way towards drawing lessons from our collaboration. My partners, Christophe Angoulvant, Patrick Biecheler, Pierre Reboul and Anne Bioulac, have all been invaluable sounding boards: I am grateful to them for corroborating my ideas and reviewing early drafts. Any mistakes that remain are my own.

I also want to thank the academics with whom I have had the chance to discuss my ideas, particularly Dean John A. Quelch of CEIBS, Prof. Peter Williamson of Cambridge Judge Business School (both of whom taught me at Harvard Business School), Dean Xian Bing of CKGSB and Prof. David Garvin of Harvard Business School. They were generous with their time and made constructive suggestions that have helped me to refine my thesis.

I owe a deep debt of gratitude to my staff in Shanghai and Beijing for their enthusiastic help during the project, particularly to Shelley Zhang, my assistant in my Asia Headquarters in Shanghai, for her supremely efficient scheduling and administration. Thanks too to my assistant in Paris, Christine Huntzinger, who manages the Sino-French life of a peripatetic consultant with great skill and unfailing charm.

Thanks also to Christiane Diekmann for helping to keep the project on track and for her enthusiastic support throughout as well as to Torsten Oltmanns for backing the book before it was clear to anyone, including myself, what it would turn out to be.

Very special thanks are due to Tom Lloyd. In addition to helping me with the writing, Tom was an excellent sparring partner as well as a diligent challenger and provider of input. We both enjoyed the journey of discovering the VUCA world: we think alike and can exchange ideas and challenge each other when necessary.

Finally, my thanks to Vafa Payman at Bloomsbury for agreeing to publish the book, to his colleague, Alana Clogan, for her patience, and to Jane Hood for her accurate, light footprint editing.

Preface

This book didn't start out this way. My original plan was to write a book about Accelerated Zero-Based Budgeting (AZBB), a consulting product we had developed at Roland Berger by accident in the summer of 2003. It had been such a success that in May 2012 colleagues suggested that we should write a book about it.

Later that summer, a client and friend asked me what I thought the next big thing would be in management. He was a great fan of AZBB. He said it was 'powerful'. But he thought most of the conventional ideas and models and some new ones – he mentioned Smart Simplicity – seemed to be missing the point, somehow. They weren't addressing the new challenges he and other managers were facing. My friend is as interested in art and philosophy as he is in business. I knew his question encompassed more than economics. For him, the next big thing would have to address the spiritual and emotional, as well as the rational and material, impacts on ordinary people of such aspects of the modern world as time-lag compression and ubiquitous acceleration.

I had no answer at the time, but I found his question intriguing.

I asked our Infocenter to find material on the history of acronyms and products in management consulting. They sent me a large stack of reading matter, which I waded through on a flight from Shanghai to Paris in September 2012.

I saw what my friend meant: I had a reasonably good understanding of what he saw as his main challenges and there was nothing in my pile of articles that seemed to offer much help. I decided to read one more article before abandoning my research and going to sleep.

My first thought, on reading the opening paragraphs, was that this article had slipped into my pile of reading material by accident.

I had been interested for some time in the US military's acronym VUCA (Volatile, Uncertain, Complex, Ambiguous) as a description of the new context of warfare. We had used it successfully with some clients as a way to characterise the new context for business and had published an article about it in Roland Berger's 2011 year-end booklet. In August 2012, a Stanford alumnus who had read the piece in a French magazine sent me an article about Barack Obama's so-called 'Light Footprint' military doctrine. It caught my eye, but since I had had no time to read it then and there, it was copied and included in my usual pile of reading for the flight to China.

This was the interloper article. I read it and, seven miles high, on the edge of sleep, things slotted into place. In a VUCA-world Light Footprint (LFP) was the answer my client was seeking – the answer for business as well for the military. It was why AZBB had been so surprisingly successful; it was part of a solution to a problem we were all facing. Other ideas came crowding in: the book on Chinese management I had published two years previously, the challenges of speed, 'big data' and human commitment. The glitches in the matrix of business that conventional management ideas seemed unable to explain suddenly became explicable and, therefore, manageable.

I don't pretend there is anything radically new about LFP. But for me, a consultant who has visited over 50 countries, worked for clients in 20 of them, and who has lived in the US, the UK, France and China it has been an epiphany that has given a new clarity to the previously confusing relationships in the VUCA world between structure, strategy, tactics, operations and leadership.

I hope it does something similar for readers.

Charles-Edouard Bouée
Shanghai
February 2013

Introduction

To say that part of a company leader's job is to ensure his or her organization adapts appropriately to a changing environment, is to state the obvious. Without thinking of it in that way managers are constantly nudging, guiding, tuning and cajoling their businesses or organizations into better fits with their environment. When their efforts are successful, their companies survive and thrive.

The trouble is that these days adaptation is not easy. There is so much to adapt to, and it has become impossible to ensure that an adaptation in one part of the business won't have knock-on effects in another, varying from the merely inconvenient to the disastrous.

But changing nothing, or changing very little, isn't an option.

Everything must be flexible now. There can be no sacred cows or 'no go' areas. In an environment growing more volatile, uncertain, complex and ambiguous by the day, the whole organization must adapt constantly. Organizational structure, routines and habits of mind, processes, business models, assumptions, approaches, modes of operation, and conventional wisdoms; all must play their part in meeting the adaptive challenge. No stone can be left unturned. Nothing can be taken for granted.

In some cases this requires looking back. The conventional idea of a 'strategy' as a plan is less relevant in the new world than the old concept of the 'strategus' as an army with a leader. And although Unique Selling Points and Value Propositions are of limited use in a world where nothing remains unique for long, a deep-seated brand identity can be a raft of stability in storm-tossed seas.

The changes in the environment have become very demanding. Harvard Business School professor John Kotter believes they 'will force us all to evolve toward a fundamentally new form of organization' - a form better suited to an unpredictable, fast-changing environment.

We're entering unchartered territory that is, at once, frightening and dangerous, but also beautiful and exciting.

In the Chinese culture, change is a stream of events flowing on forever. But above the stream there are immutable laws ruling all change. This is the 'Dao', the way, the circle of light and dark, the *yin* and the *yang*.

This book will argue that right now, in the early 21st century, the Dao for business, the way to the new form of organization demanded by today's environment, is the quality of 'lightness'. This is not to be confused with the quality of 'simplicity', a quest for which can be hazardous in a complex world where nothing is quite what it seems.

The adaptive theme for organizations of all kinds is shedding mass and weight; doing more and more with less and less. Being lighter has a number of attractions in a volatile, unpredictable world. It makes an organization more agile, accurate and precise in its movements; by shedding low grade work, it increases value-added per employee; it allows the organization to tread more lightly and so cause less disruption.

The book draws inspiration from two unconventional sources. Barack Obama's 'light footprint' military doctrine, and what the author has elsewhere called China's 'management revolution'. Both are of interest to western civilian organizations, for different reasons. The former is a pure, no-holds-barred, no-expense-spared response to the challenge of 'Protecting America' in a turbulent world. The latter is a real-life experiment in how business organizations and management approaches evolve in such a world.

The book begins in Chapter 1 with a brief survey of the origins of the conventional management wisdoms, and the roles played in their evolution by business schools and management consulting firms. The chapter goes on to suggest the conventional wisdoms are struggling to accommodate recent changes in the business environment and that 'glitches in the matrix' are occurring that suggest the need for a new conceptual framework.

Chapter 2 describes the competitive dynamics of the 'arms race' in the military domain, suggests the same dynamics drive competition in the business area, and argues that three components of Barack Obama's 'light footprint' military doctrine (use of drones, cyber weapons and special forces) can, therefore, be seen as presages of business competition.

The question of why the US has adopted a light footprint approach to warfare is addressed in Chapter 3. The answer proposed is that it was invoked by VUCA (Volatile, Uncertain, Complex, Ambiguous); the acronym used by the American military to summarise the main features of its operating environment. VUCA is then related to the sciences of complexity, and complex adaptive systems, and it is argued that it also characterises today's operating environment for business.

It is suggested in Chapter 4 that the new management style emerging in China should also be seen by western company managers as a presage, because, unlike the occidental management approach that traced its origins back to the US in the mid-19th century, it began its evolutionary journey at the dawn of the VUCA age and therefore should be seen as having been invoked by VUCA to some extent.

Informed by these military and Chinese 'presages' Chapter 5 begins to explore their implications for management. Business equivalents of these three light footprint stratagems are described and elements of the approach detected in the Daoist management style of Apple's Steve Jobs.

Chapter 6 focuses on four distinctive characteristics of the Light Footprint (LFP) organization: its structure, which is at once both centralised and decentralised; its propensity to collaborate with, rather than hire or acquire, others, and its associated predisposition to trust; its reliance on surprise as a competitive weapon; its awareness of all the consequences of its actions.

The LFP organization is seen in Chapter 7 as being balanced on the edge of instability and as reconciling a number dualisms: hope and fear; change and continuity; the vertical and the horizontal; the individual and the organization. Its essence, and the focal point of its management, is its organizational or 'Gemba' power (as it's known in Japan). And the LFP organization is 'data friendly'.

Chapter 8 contrasts the management approach in an LFP organization with conventional management, and uses a recently developed, high-speed management tool, Accelerated Zero-Based Budgeting (AZBB), as an example of a VUCA-adapted management intervention.

It is suggested in Chapter 9 that the LFP organization requires an 'enlightened' leadership style. Enlightened leaders focus on what their organizations are, rather than what they would like them to be. They are aware of the prevailing social and political contexts of business. They take an essentially pragmatic approach.

In the final chapter, the argument is summarized and 10 practical steps are described for the gradual, piecemeal transformation of a conventional organization into an LFP organization.

Adaptation is, of necessity, a piecemeal process. The organization is, by definition, already well-adapted. Major changes are almost sure to be disadvantageous. The 'Hopeful Monster' and other non-gradualist theories of evolution have never successfully countered the objection of Darwinian gradualists; namely that a mutant won't survive in an environment to which its parents are adapted, unless it is very similar to its parents.

The LFP organization is very like a conventional organization; the differences are more a matter of emphasis, than substance; more to do with philosophy, than structure. But these marginal differences all add up, if not to the 'fundamentally new form of organization' John Kotter advocates, at least to something that feels different to those who work for it, and deal with it as customers, suppliers or partners – it feels lighter, quicker, more agile, more trusting and more worthy of trust.

The focus in the pages that follow is on business institutions and networks, but LFP-type organizations are likely to spread beyond the business and military worlds; the VUCA qualities that are invoking them are becoming evident in all walks of life and in every institutional nook and cranny.

Chapter 1

Unfit for purpose

There is something wrong with conventional management wisdoms and with the way the arts and sciences of management are taught these days. Their concepts and models don't seem as useful as they once were and the assumptions and principles on which management thinking rests seem less plausible. It is as if the development of the management theories has reached some temporal or spatial limit; that they are out of date, or less generally applicable than was thought.

To get an idea of what might have gone wrong with what the English biologist C. H. Waddington called the 'conventional wisdom of the dominant group' (COWDUNG) in management, we need to recall where it has come from.

Its origins lie in the mid-19th century and the birth of the modern company on the American railroads. As the distinguished historian Alfred Chandler pointed out in his Pulitzer prize-winning book *The Visible Hand*, the birth of the 'multi-unit business enterprise', as he called it, was a response to an accident on the Western Railroad on October 5, 1841. According Chandler, the implementation of the structural recommendations inspired by the accident created, 'the first modern, carefully defined, internal organizational structure used by an American business enterprise' and, 'the first [company] . . . to operate through a formal administrative structure, manned by full-time salaried managers'.[1]

Chandler argued that the multi-unit business enterprise (MUBE) and its managerial system were invoked by circumstances: by 'the rapid pace of technological innovation and increasing consumer demand in the US during the second half of the nineteenth century'.

But it didn't emerge unique or fully formed. It inherited many of its characteristics from existing organizations, particularly the military. Its hierarchical shape aped the military's class system, which concentrates power at the top, and its system of bureaucracy was based on that of the 'armed' European trading companies of the 17th and 18th centuries (see box below).

European trading companies

In December 1600, England's Queen Elizabeth I granted a charter to 'The Governor and Company of Merchants of London Trading into the East Indies', conferring on them a trading monopoly in Asia, Africa and America. The only restriction imposed was that the company should not contest the existing trading rights of 'any Christian prince'.

The new company was managed by a governor and 24 directors, chosen from wealthy aristocratic investors trading with 'joint stock'. On its early voyages, it ventured as far as Japan, but established its first 'factories' (trading posts, run by 'factors') in Madras and Bombay in 1610 and 1611 respectively. Having absorbed several rival companies and acquired more rights from the Crown, the English East India Company (EEIC) established itself as a major power in India at the end of the 17th century.

In retrospect, the EEIC and the other European trading companies of the time can be seen as proto-companies, as the agents of mercantilist states. They were part trading companies, part private armies, using military power to secure and protect commercial interests.

The EEIC became the dominant power in India following the victories of the EEIC officer, Robert Clive, over the French at Arcot in 1751 and the Bengali prince, Suraj-ud-Dowlah (perpetrator of the 'Black Hole of Calcutta' massacre), at Plassey in 1757.

After Plassey, the EEIC had a monopoly in the production of Indian opium and saw China as an attractive market, despite the fact that the drug had been prohibited in China since 1729. The EEIC evaded the ban by buying tea in Canton (Guangzhou) on credit, offsetting these debts by selling opium at auction in Calcutta (Kolkata), and then smuggling the narcotic into China.

The Qing government re-affirmed the prohibition in 1799, and again in 1810. By 1838 the British (by then, the EEIC had lost its monopolies of the Indian and Chinese trades) were smuggling 1,400 tons of opium a year into China. The first Opium War broke out the following year after the emperor tried, unsuccessfully, to enforce the ban.

Some senior EEIC 'officers' became so fabulously rich during their tours of Indian duty that they acquired the nickname 'nabobs' (the English version of the Indian 'nawab'). Clive amassed a fabulous personal fortune before his 35th birthday. His share of the reparations for the Black Hole of Calcutta massacre extracted after the battle of Plassey was £90m in today's money, and that was not the half of his wealth.

But military prowess was no defence against the EEIC's position as the chartered holder of sovereign rights. Its charter was renewed several times during the 18th century, but each time it was obliged to make financial concessions to the Crown. In 1773, government appointed Warren Hastings the governor-general of India and greatly reduced the company's adminis-trative role. An 'India Department' of the British government was created by the 1784 India Act, to assume political, military and financial control of the EEIC's affairs.

The company continued to play a significant administrative role in India until the Sepoy Mutiny of 1857-8, but the Act for the Better Government of India of 1858 transferred its governmental duties to the Crown and absorbed its 24,000 troops into the British Army. On January 1, 1874 the company was finally dissolved by the East India Stock Dividend Redemption Act.

The MUBE has been the focus of the evolution of management thought and of two other groups of institutions – the business schools and management consultancies – that serve them, ever since.

Business schools

As Harvard Business School professor John Kotter has pointed out, the new companies began complaining about shortages of qualified staff to run their organizations as early as the 1860s.[2]

The University of Pennsylvania responded to this skill shortage in 1881 by founding the Wharton School of Finance and Commerce, which offered an undergraduate 'management' degree. Similar schools were set up in California, Chicago and elsewhere before the end of the 19th century. In 1908 the Harvard Business School (HBS) was founded to offer a master's degree in business administration (MBA).

George Baker, head of what would become Citicorp, was impressed by the Harvard school and in 1925 gave it the money to construct an eight-building campus. The following year, 58,000 students, taught by 2,500 faculty at 132 American schools, majored in business. Most of them joined large companies on graduation.

It was inevitable, given the inspirations for the schools and the destinations of their graduates, that intimate relationships would develop between the 'B-schools', as they are now known, and large companies. This was particularly true at HBS. The library is named after George Baker, the MBA classrooms are Aldrich and Rockefeller (Standard Oil), the dining hall is Kresge (K-Mart), the executive programs are taught in Cumnock (J. P. Stevens) and the main office building is Morgan (Morgan Guaranty and Stanley).

The American business schools played a vital role in the evolution of managerial capitalism and of the 'practice' of management. They provided the skills Chandler's MUBEs needed and became the main repositories of management knowledge and the principal laboratories for research, as well as key hubs for the development of management models, principles and techniques.

But the business school has long since ceased to be an exclusively US institution.

According to the *Financial Times* 'Global MBA rankings' of business schools, half of the top 100 by starting salaries of MBA graduates in 2012 were in the US, 13 were in the UK, five were in Canada and four were in China. Spain had three. Australia, France, India and Switzerland had two each, and several other countries had one. The erosion of US dominance will continue as new schools are opened.

Three of China's top four business schools are in Hong Kong, the China Europe International Business School (CEIBS, China's second-ranked school) is in Shanghai, and the Cheung Kong Graduate School of Business (CKGSB – see box opposite) is based in Beijing.

Cheung Kong Graduate School of Business

The Cheung Kong Graduate School of Business (CKGSB) was established with an endowment from the Li Ka-shing Foundation in 2002. Based in Beijing, it has campuses in Shanghai and Guangzhou as well as offshoots in London and New York.

CKGSB is distinctive in China in several respects. It charges much higher fees than other Chinese business schools, runs a programme for chief executives and has an unusually illustrious faculty. Although most of its professors are ethnic Chinese, they have studied and taught at some of the world's leading business schools and are publishing research in academic journals at a rate comparable with those of the top 20 business schools worldwide.

In explaining his reasons for founding the school, Li Ka-shing, one of China's wealthiest businessmen and the chairman of Cheung Kong (Holdings) and Hutchison Whampoa says on the CKGSB website (www.cheungkong-gsb.com).

> While traditional Confucian philosophy stresses high moral standards, the majority of contemporary business management courses regard business efficiency and profitability as the criteria by which to measure the success of corporations. Neither of these two value systems reflects the entirety of business values . . . true success [in business] requires a blending of value systems.

(A declaration of interest is necessary here – the author sits on the CKGSB advisory board.)

Management consultants

Arthur D. Little, the roots of which date back to 1886, claims to be 'the oldest management consulting firm in the world'. But, as Dr. Dietmar Fink, Professor of Management Consulting and Corporate Development at the Bonn-Rhein-Sieg University of Applied Sciences, has pointed out, it is more accurate to call it 'the oldest company that has . . . developed into a management consultancy in the modern sense of the word'.

Under the name Griffin and Little, Chemical Engineers Arthur Dehon Little and Roger Griffin analyzed chemicals, metals and foodstuffs for businesses at a time when product purity was a major concern. A century later, consultants would do good business responding to a similar concern: product quality.

Another key date in the annals of consulting is April 9, 1930 when an article about a new type of advisor, a 'management consultant', by James O. McKinsey, a professor of business at the University of Chicago, was published in *Business Week* magazine.

The world economy was in crisis and many companies were teetering on the brink. Banks and investment houses had reluctantly taken control of their debtors' businesses, and turned to advisors for help in turning them round. Among these advisors was the Cleveland law firm Jones Day. Since many of the tasks entrusted to Jones Day were more to do with business than the law, Jones Day asked one of their employees, Harvard graduate Marvin Bower, to handle these clients.

Previously, these turn-round cases had focused mainly on financial and legal issues, rather than on the management failings that had caused the problems in the first place. Bower felt a specialized company was needed to address management issues professionally. In 1932 he met James McKinsey.

McKinsey's distinctive 'value proposition' was that his firm could not only help unhealthy firms become efficient, it could also help healthy firms reach their full potential. In 1929 he took on his first partner, Andrew Kearney, the former director of market research at one of his clients. In 1932, when McKinsey met Bower, he had 15 partners and had just opened a second office in New York where he offered Bower a job.

Demand for consultants was high during the post-crash recovery and was given an added stimulus by the 1933 Glass-Steagall Act, which forced the separation of commercial banks from securities firms in the US and barred banks from business advisory and reorganization activities.

After a less than successful time as CEO of the Chicago department store, Marshall Field's, McKinsey died in 1937 and his old firm was reorganized along lines proposed by Bower, now number two in the New York office, under Horace G. Crockett. A new firm, McKinsey & Company, took over the loss-making offices in Boston and New York and the Chicago partners operated under the name McKinsey, Kearney & Company.

Bower was the architect of the reorganization and, in the codes of behaviour, language and dress he stipulated for the new East Coast practice, of the modern management consulting firm.

The industry had a good war. In the 1950s, consolidation led to the emergence of three firms: Booz, Allen & Hamilton; Cresap, McCormick & Paget; and McKinsey & Co. as market leaders. In the early 1960s they opened offices in Europe and before long, US firms selling US management practices dominated the global consulting market.

In 1963, Bruce Henderson, the head of management services at Arthur D. Little, was asked by The Boston Safe Deposit and Trust Company to form a consulting department. Henderson accepted the invitation and, within a year, the fledgling Boston Consulting Group (BCG) was employing six consultants. Henderson felt the young firm needed an edge in the increasingly competitive market and positioned BCG as a 'strategy' consultancy (see below).

The origins of strategy

The Greek word στρατηγός is a combination of 'stratos' (army), and 'ago' (lead/guide/move). In Roman times a 'strategus' was a commander-in-chief or chief magistrate. A 'strategy' was an army or province under a 'strategus'. Later it came to mean the art of a strategus, or the function and tasks of a general or commander-in-chief.

The word retained this meaning until Count Guibert, the French military thinker, introduced the term 'La Stratégique' in 1799. In the 19th century von Clausewitz defined it as 'the use of fighting for the purpose of war'. His most illustrious student, the Prussian general von Moltke, defined the term as 'continuing the original guiding thought, while adapting it to reflect continually changing circumstances'.

In their 1944 book *Theory of Games and Economic Behavior*, John von Neumann and Oskar Morgenstern used 'strategy' to mean a sequence of steps aimed at achieving a specified goal.[3] In the 1960s, Igor Ansoff applied the term to business management, and saw strategies as instructions derived from corporate goals. The strategy defines the overall direction and prescribes the allocation of resources.

Henderson's timing was impeccable. In both business and government, the post-war love affair with planning based on annual budgets was drawing to a close: horizons were extending. Multiyear planning based on forecasts was becoming more popular. The focus of the planning was switching from functions and business units to entire companies.

In 1967, Roland Berger founded in Germany the consulting firm that still bears his name. He took a different approach from the market leader, McKinsey, which was focusing at that time on divisional organization and cost reduction. He was an entrepreneur and wanted to help his clients become more successful. Some of the firm's major projects have involved significant mergers and acquisitions (M&A), but Berger sees himself as a strategist rather than an M&A expert, and views his firm as having grown out of the European, rather than the American, culture.

By the early 1970s, strategy consulting was the primary offering of management consultants, and the focus of consultancy marketing was switching from nurturing long-term relationships to developing new ideas, analytical tools and standardized approaches. This led to a change in the location of consulting work from the client's offices to the consultancy firm's. BCG consultants, for example, served their clients from their head office, and travelled to the client only for project meetings.

Much earlier another important development for consulting occurred when, in 1954, the accountancy firm Arthur Andersen helped General Electric install a computer system at its plant in Louisville. The 'IT' practice this project spawned prospered. During the 1970s and 1980s, its revenue growth handsomely outpaced that of the audit business. The two practices were separated in 1989 and in the wake of the collapse of the audit business after the Enron scandal, the consulting practice was re-named Accenture.

In recent years the industry has gone from feast to famine in line with the prevailing business cycle, and major business developments including globalization, the re-unification of Germany, the introduction of the Euro, the Y2K scare (the fear that computer systems all over the world would fail on New Year's Day 2000) and the forced separation of auditing and consulting.

But, throughout the post-war period, the leading strategy consulting firms have – in tandem with prominent business schools – been the co-inventors and the main distributors of new management ideas, tools, concepts and techniques.

How business ideas evolve

In his book *The Selfish Gene*, Richard Dawkins proposed the idea of 'memes', units of imitation and memory that evolve in response to adaptive challenges in much the same way as genes, by means of a process of extinction and mutation.[4]

What we call 'culture' consists of memes, of the tiny fractions of all that has been said, written and made since the humans evolved and that have survived because the succeeding generations have remembered, or kept, them. Some memes, such as the wheel, knowledge of fire and much of science, live on more or less forever and are the bedrock of our knowledge. Others, such as great literature and art, religions, music, poems and philosophies, may live for centuries. Still others, such as jokes, fashions, tweets, fads and viral videos, are ephemeral: they bloom briefly and are forgotten, for a time. They may be remembered. These days, it is very hard to forget anything entirely – even the oldest jokes, the most dated fashions and the oddest ideas live on in silicon limbo, and can be recalled at any time with a few keystrokes.

Sub-sets of these meme-built cultures can be found in all walks of life. Modern business still employs memes as ancient as language – trade, barter, price, arbitrage and, much later, money. The modern company carries the memes of joint stock and limited liability it inherited from its precursors, the national trading companies of the 17th century (see above). As noted earlier, the practice of management began to coalesce into a coherent set of memes in the mid-19th century after the emergence of the modern corporate form on US railroads. Many of its components – specialization, scale economies, out-sourcing, debt and equity financing – emerged earlier, during the Industrial Revolution. Others – such as hierarchical organizations, the designation of managers as 'officers' and the idea of corporate 'strategy' – were imported from the military, through the armed trading companies of the mercantilist era (see above).

The management meta-meme embarked on a period of rapid development in the late 19th and early 20th centuries, with the establishment of the business schools, the formation of management consultants, and the birth of 'professional managers'. The origins of the memes of mass production and Frederick Taylor's 'scientific management' can be traced back to Adam Smith's advocacy of 'specialisation' in the 18th century.

In his book, *Managing on the Edge*, Richard Pascale said, 'The very notion of "professional management" rests upon the premise that a set of generic concepts underlies managerial activity anywhere'. Pascale tracked the rise and fall of management memes or 'fads', as he called them, from 1950 to 1988 by the frequency of citations in the literature: managerial grid, decision trees, Theories X, Y and Z, T-Groups, management by objectives, experience curve, strategic business units, zero-based budgeting, value chain, excellence, re-structuring, portfolio management, quality circles, *kanban*, matrix and 'one-minute managing'.[5]

There have been some lively debates within the consulting industry over the years, as firms vied with one another to attract clients. McKinsey's 'critical success factors' model emerged from its work with General Electric where it developed the 'McKinsey/GE matrix', a three-by-three matrix that related 'industry attractiveness' to 'business strength'. BCG derived a rival two-by-two matrix from its founder Bruce Henderson's 'experience curve', which divided a company's businesses into four types: stars, cash cows, dogs, and 'question marks'. Both were designed to help clients decide how to allocate resources.

McKinsey's matrix has been characterized as 'qualitative', because it dealt with the qualities of competitiveness and attractiveness; the 'quantitative' BCG approach, on the other hand, identified attractiveness with market growth, and competitiveness with market share and thus the position on the 'experience curve'.

In the 1980s, the rivalry of the matrices gave way to 'shareholder value'. New names appeared in the consulting industry, such as Strategic Planning Associates, Marakon and Stern Stewart. This was the age of 'corporate raiders': Carl Icahn, James Goldsmith, the Belzberg brothers and Hanson Trust. The frontier of industrial development switched from the corporate boardroom to the investment banks, the analysts 'sweat shops' in the shareholder value boutiques, and the bars and backrooms frequented by the dealmakers. Businesses became tradable commodities. It was eat, or be eaten – capitalism 'red in tooth and claw'.

Then came Michael Porter and the return of Harvard Business School as the main strategy laboratory. The focus of attention switched from shareholders back to industries. Porter's assertion that five forces determine an industry's profitability – internal rivalry, the bargaining power of suppliers and customers, the threat of new entrants and substitute products – and low-cost strategies weren't always appropriate, refuted the primacy BCG had assigned to market share and the 'experience curve.'

In 1989, a new model appeared in the form of the 'Strategic Intent and Core Competencies' ideas of C.K. Prahalad and Gary Hamel. They said that existing strategic models were wrong, because all relied on some kind of market segmentation for business units and took no account of the power of human intent to re-shape industries. This was why, Prahalad and Hamel claimed, Japanese companies had won most of the competitive battles in the consumer electronics and car markets.

Since then many more TLAs (three letter acronyms) have had time in the management literature limelight: ABC (activity-based costing), BPR (business process re-engineering), BSC (balanced scorecard), ERP (enterprise resource planning – a meme that took physical form in software packages), CRM (customer relationship management), and CSR (corporate social responsibility).

It's not as simple as that, of course. The dwindling and cessation of literature citations does not necessarily mean decline and extinction. Some management memes stop attracting the attention of the literature not because they have fallen into disuse, but because they have proved so useful that they have become commonplace and thus unremarkable, or because old ideas re-emerge in different forms, or under different names. W. Edwards Deming's 'statistical quality control', foreshadowed in 'scientific management', changed manufacturing permanently by commoditising quality. It spawned the 'quality circle', and morphed into TQM (total quality management).

Other management memes that drop out of the limelight, because of their practical weaknesses or a loss of relevance, can sometimes have 'second comings' when, for instance, a change in the business environment restores their lost relevance or when their weaknesses prove remediable.

Taken together, the application of these theories has improved management beyond all recognition since the birth of the modern company in the 19th century. But by and large, these improvements have been incremental. The current interest in 'lean', for instance, can be seen as simply the latest instalment in occidental managers' long, on-off love affair with Japanese management principles that can trace its origins back to Deming, TQM and the Toyota Production System (TPS). At one level it can be seen as a philosophy that exhorts managers not to waste money or time on inefficient procedures and superfluous processes and to recognize and try constantly to honour their duty to shareholders in order to deliver the best possible products at the lowest possible cost. At another level it is simply a set of tools for eliminating waste (or *muda*, as the Japanese call it).

The nearest approach to the breakthroughs that occur from time to time in the development of science and warfare was the shareholder value revolution in the mid 1980s (see above).

It was, as much as anything else, a phenomenological revolution, a clear and simple specification, perhaps for the first time (or was it just a reminder?), of the fundamental purpose of companies: to create value for shareholders. It was an accurate description of a company's situational logic and 'managing for value' remains, for that reason, an important part of the modern management canon.

But it was not a successful revolution, because, coinciding as it did with the de-regulation of the financial services industry, it led to intensive 'gaming' with shareholder value and, perversely, to a dramatic shift in the distribution of value from shareholders to managers.

To be specific, it encouraged company boards to inundate their CEOs with share options and other equity-based incentives so that they would become, if the companies' shares rose substantially, wealthy beyond the dreams of avarice.

In the financial services sector this had two consequences: higher dependence on debt and aggressive incentive arrangements for sales staff designed to ensure the targets in senior executive Long-term Incentive Plans were met.

If it was a real breakthrough, it was one that nearly broke the system.

Glitches in the matrix

Companies managed in accordance with the ideas, models, principles and techniques prescribed by the business schools, and refined and applied by their distributors, the management consultants, are, to a large extent, the creators of the modern world. They dominate the international *Fortune 500* list and their brands are in demand everywhere. There is no disputing the success of the search by the business schools and the leading management consultants for better ways to manage large, multi-unit business enterprises.

But strange things are happening these days that seem at odds with the management *oeuvre*. Together they are reminiscent of a scene in the science-fiction film, *The Matrix*.

The protagonist, Neo, sees a black cat walk by, and then he sees a similar black cat walk by.

'Whoa,' he says. 'Déjà vu.'

'What did you just say?' asks Trinity.

'Nothing. Just had a little déjà vu.'

'What did you see?'

. . .

'A black cat went past us, and then another that looked just like it.'

'How much like it? Was it the same cat?'

'It might have been. I'm not sure . . . What is it?'

'A déjà vu is usually a glitch in the Matrix. It happens when they change something.'

The glitches hinted at the truth: that what appeared to be reality was actually a virtual world, overlaying and obscuring reality. It is a bit like that with management thinking right now. Glitches in the world as the contemporary management *oeuvre* or COWDUNG sees it suggest the existence or emergence of a different or a new reality beneath the COWDUNG veneer.

Some of these glitches are associated with changes in recent years in the geographical distribution of the world's largest companies. From 2001 to 2011, the number of North American-based companies in *Fortune* magazine's *Global 500* rankings fell from 215 to 146, while the number of Asian companies increased from 116 to 172. In the 2012 *Global 500* ranking, there were 132 US companies and 73 Chinese companies.

The emergence of Japan as a major industrial power – and of Japanese companies as world leaders in auto making and consumer electronics in the second half of the 20th century – had a profound and lasting influence on Western management thinking and practice. It would be surprising if the impact of the rise of China and of its companies in the first half of the 21st century is less profound (see Chapter 4).

But not all the glitches in the management matrix are consequences of the influx of non-western business cultures.

Free

According to Michael Porter, the competitiveness of an industry is determined by, among other things, the threat of new entrants. If profit margins are 'too high', other players are attracted in and profit margins fall to 'normal' levels.

But what do 'too high' and 'normal' mean? At any one time they are reflections of a consensus within the industry about standards for production efficiency, product quality, marketing and other costs, capital expenditure, and pricing. In a competitive industry, the leaders do a little better than average, the laggards do a little worse. Since no player earns 'abnormal' profits, there's nothing to attract new entrants.

Unless, of course, a new entrant comes along who either doesn't know the rules and standards or blithely ignores them. William Shockley destroyed the thermionic valve industry by inventing transistors; Henry Ford created a mass market for cars by re-inventing the method of their manufacture; Michael Dell revolutionized the retailing of PCs; the cut-price airlines did for air travel what Henry Ford had done for cars; Steve Jobs reinvented the mobile phone.

Until early 2012, French mobile phone services were among the most expensive in Europe and local operators enjoyed a relatively high average revenue per user (ARPU). French broadband services, on the other hand, were among the cheapest in Europe, thanks largely to a maverick entrepreneur, Xavier Niel, an iconoclastic product of the early Internet culture who traded heavy, industry-standard marketing budgets for lower prices for customers.

In 2002, Niel's Internet service provider (ISP) company, Free, set a cat among the ISP pigeons by offering a triple-play service with DSL Internet, unlimited VoIP calls (voice over Internet) to French landline phones, and television for €29.99 a month.

Free's pricing policy was also its marketing policy. As its competitors hired large sales teams and invested heavily in advertising, Free remained price leader and, increasingly, value leader as it added, for instance, a Video on Demand portal and a high tech decoder. It enjoyed far lower customer acquisition costs than its competitors and came to be seen as a consumer advocate, as well as a service provider. In the end, Free's competitors had no choice but to follow its pricing structure and make do with lower margins.

When the French ISP market consolidated, three players, Orange, SFR and Bouygues Telecom, emerged as market leaders. Free remained an odd-ball outlier, but no-one expected it to survive for long after the three main players, all integrated telco groups, bundled their triple-play ISP offers with mobile phone plans. You could almost hear the sighs of relief from the three key players as they prepared to restore their ISP margins.

Relief turned to alarm in 2009 when the Autorité de régulation des communications électroniques et des postes (ARCEP), the industry's regulator, decided three mobile phone providers were not enough to ensure healthy competition and sold a fourth licence to Free. The licence required Free to negotiate a 2G roaming agreement with another operator. Free finally secured a 3G roaming agreement with Orange.

Far from leaving the troublesome Niel behind with an ISP market he had low-balled almost to death, the three telco incumbents saw him and his alarming ideas coming at them in their core businesses.

Niel began taunting them right away, promising to revolutionize the mobile phone market in France with unlimited offers for a fraction of the price. But it took him a while to get set up.

First, he had to finance the heavy, front-end investment needed to build a mobile network that, as required by the terms of Free's licence, provided at least 25% coverage of the total population at launch. A conventional company would have asked a bank for a loan. Niel turned to his ISP customers. He bundled unlimited VoIP calls to mobile phones with his Internet package and slightly raised the price when VAT changes came into effect. The higher margins on the ISP package generated higher cash flow for investing in the mobile network.

Second, Free cut its front-end investment in two ways: by building its cell towers very far apart and incorporating Free's Internet 'hotspot' network, among the largest in the world, into the mobile network.

To conventional mobile operators, it was an extremely unconventional minimalist network that sacrificed comprehensive coverage for low front-end costs. Others saw it as a glitch in the mobile matrix; as a highly sophisticated re-writing of the rules of the conventional mobile game that used the smartphone to fuse Internet and mobile networks together.

The proof of the pudding would be in the eating.

With Niel claiming that the three incumbent operators were milking their customers dry (by charging €45 to €65 a month for smartphone plans with only a couple of hours of talk time), Free announced its mobile package in January 2012. It was a dream for customers, but a nightmare for the incumbents – unlimited talk, unlimited SMS and MMS messages, tethering, unlimited data and no contract all for €19.99 a month.

Since the Free package offers no discount on phone, it was hard to compare the packages directly. But the headline monthly charge for a wholly unlimited multi-play deal was too striking to ignore. The incumbents had to respond. Within months all three offered similar deals for €20–25 a month, thus corroborating Niel's accusation that until Free's arrival they had been milking their customers.

Free played the price card again by launching a €2 a month package offering one hour of call time plus 60 texts. This has effectively put paid to the prepaid market in France.

It has also offered discounts for Free's ISP customers: €16.99 for the full mobile package, or the minimal, one hour call package for free. This has led to a substantial influx of new ISP customers.

Within six months, Free had 5.4% of the mobile market – 3.6 million customers. By the end of 2012, the figure was up to 5 million (7.5% market share). Since the French market is virtually saturated most of these must have been seduced by its prices and by its maverick, youthful brand, and so away from the incumbents. There are some sceptics, however. Some predict that, having made a splash at launch, Niel will find it harder to maintain growth and generate the money needed to finance necessary capital expenditure.

But it may be premature to report the end of Free's mould-breaking reign. The company is innovative, ingenious, opportunistic and quick on its feet. It is better adapted than its competitors to the modern environment and more aware of the possibilities that lie between, as well as within the latest technologies. Although younger and smaller than its rivals, it seems more street-wise; more in tune with what people want, and what technology allows them to have.

Niel has been up to his David and Goliath antics again. In January 2013 Free changed the software on the modems it supplies to its 5 million ISP customers, so that online advertisements were blocked by default. The move, thought to have been aimed at Google, with whom Free was reported to have been in talks about whether it will pay for access to Free's customers, challenged the standard single ISP revenue stream model.[6]

Like Sir Richard Branson's Virgin group, only more so, Free is more than a brand. Its iconoclasm, its refusal to take the *status quo* for granted, and its frontal assault on profiteering incumbents in the markets it enters, not to mention its pricing, attract people – particularly young people. It's acquiring some of the qualities of a social movement.

Straws in the wind

The sudden collapse of the strategy consulting firm, Monitor Group, in November 2012 was a glitch that caused great alarm within management consulting.

Forensic experts immediately began anxiously to examine the corpse in search of the cause of death of the consultancy firm co-founded by Michael Porter in 1983 to package and sell his ideas.

The consensus view seems to be that Monitor failed because demand for its Porteresque offerings, based on the assumption that firms could achieve a 'sustainable competitive advantage' by exploiting structural imperfections in their industries, dried up.

Writing in *Forbes* soon after Monitor's collapse, Steve Denning said that the bankruptcy 'marked the beginning of the end of the era of business metaphysics and the exposure of the most over-valued idea on the planet: sustainable competitive advantage'.[7]

But it would be wrong to accuse Porter himself of being stuck in a 30-year rut. In what amounts to another glitch in the conventional management wisdom, he has placed the company seeking a sustainable competitive advantage in a social context. In two *Harvard Business Review* articles, written with Mark Kramer of the Kennedy School at Harvard University,[8] Porter has been developing the familiar notion of 'corporate social responsibility' (CSR) into the general idea of 'shared value'.

As one arch-priest of strategy has been acknowledging the need for the strategist to recognize a social context, another, Gary Hamel, has been acknowledging by implication at least that strategy-led management thinking has paid insufficient attention in the past to the importance of speed and innovation. In his latest book *What Matters Now: How to Win in a World of Relentless Change, Ferocious Competition, and Unstoppable Innovation*, Hamel says that companies these days must be large, but also flexible; disciplined, but also 'empowered'; focused, but also opportunistic; principled, but also pragmatic; rational, but also intuitive.[9]

Another straw in the wind blowing around the strategy epicentre of Harvard Business School is HBS Professor John Kotter's proposal that firms should use 'parallel operating systems', because traditional hierarchies and processes can't identify opportunities and threats early enough and can't respond to them quickly enough (see Chapter 3).[10]

These recent revisions to strategy-centric positions do not amount to recantations, but they do indicate a certain doubt within the management establishment about the fit of conventional management wisdoms to the modern business environment.

Lacklustre times

Another glitch, not in the matrix itself, but in the political and social environment from which companies derive their licences to operate, is the recent breakdown of the unwritten contract between ordinary people, and those running the system.

In the firestorm of recrimination and accusation that followed the 2007–08 crash, the trust ordinary people had had in 'The-Powers-That-Be' and their tolerance of the astronomical pay packets of company bosses and investment bankers were severely damaged.

While the system seemed to be running well and general standards of living were rising, people tolerated the rapidly growing inequalities and the huge sums paid to CEOs, hedge fund managers and investment bankers. When the system crashed, however, they were incensed by the 'golden parachutes' paid to ex-CEOs who had contributed to the crash and were outraged when, *faute de mieux*, their money was used to rescue the banks that had precipitated the crisis.

The financial crisis also exposed a profoundly unfair asymmetry in the system. In a rising market, bank lending magnifies gains, which enrich a few hedge fund managers, investment bankers and top-level executives. But in a falling market, it magnifies losses, which are carried by everyone when banks are bailed out by the taxpayer. 'In this way,' as William Jacobson neatly put it in his letter to the *Financial Times* on November 10, 2008, 'gains are privatised while losses are socialised, and, cycle after cycle, the distribution of wealth becomes more and more unequal'.

As time passed, it became clear to ordinary people that this was no temporary blip. On the contrary, the pre-crash lending binge had condemned everyone, particularly in the West, to a decade or more of austerity budgets and falling living standards. People watched in bemusement as ever more skeletons emerged from the cupboard. As well as enriching themselves inordinately, bankers had been laundering drug money and cheating, by fixing the important London Interbank Offer Rate, for example. Companies had also been avoiding tax by routing their earnings through low-tax jurisdictions.

These problems do not call liberal capitalism itself into question as a system for allocating resources. They are not fundamental in that sense and can be fixed with tighter regulation and better oversight. But it will not be easy to re-build public trust in the system.

The system is not broken but it appears so, and no one seems to know how to mend it. European politicians cannot agree on how to mend the common currency system, and, at the time of writing, US politicians seemed to be blithely indifferent to the anxieties of their constituents as they played chicken with one another on the edge of a so-called 'fiscal cliff'.

In these lacklustre times, when people have lost their faith in the competence of their leaders, and in the system that determines the division of created value; when distrust and resentment is rife in the relationships between the economic classes, and accusations of unfairness and lack of accountability abound; when our politicians squabble, while living standards fall; when our companies are seen to have been hijacked by a predatory, amoral elite bent on their own enrichment at the expense of employees, savers and pensioners; and when our institutions seem out-dated and incapable of managing our economies and societies at a time of unprecedented turbulence and uncertainty, there is a hunger for a 'new deal'.

Voters made aware by the bail-out of 'too-big-to-fail' banks that they have been played as fools in a 'heads I win, tails you lose' game, will insist on such a 'new deal'. It would be folly for them to allow the current game to continue as it is. In democracies it is ultimately up to the people to decide the kinds of society they want to live in and the kinds of organization they want to work in and for.

Companies live among people; their organizational or 'Gemba' power consists of people, and people everywhere are looking for enlightenment and a new vision of the good life. They are waking up from a dark age, when the company was seen as merely an engine for creating shareholder value, and realizing that the world has become complex and confusing. They are searching for visions to hang on to and be guided by.

Some are looking upwards to a divine authority for guiding visions and rules by which to live their lives. Some are looking downwards to the earth beneath their feet – to the natural, the organic, the 'green'. Some are looking back to a simpler world, where ideas and ideals were clearer and less equivocal. Some are looking forwards to a new synthesis that reconciles or transcends all the confusing and conflicting themes of modern life.

In China, for example, there is a debate within the ruling Chinese Communist Party (CCP) between 'conservatives', associated with the disgraced politburo member, Bo Xilai, who draw on Mao Zedong for inspiration, and the progressive 'Shanghai set'. There is also a debate between Chinese entrepreneurs still wedded to an American model of business and those feeling their way towards a synthesis of western management and a more spiritual, Chinese, approach.

It's hard to overestimate the power of a compelling vision. When the young Henry Kissinger was asked by President Harry Truman what he had learned during his time as an adviser to Franklin Roosevelt, Kissinger said he had learned that Presidents are subject to many constraints. Truman hired him, but told him Presidents can do a lot more than they think if they have a vision. Jack Kennedy was a case in point. His vision of sending a man to the Moon was wishful thinking when he announced it, but alternately the vision was realized.

Voltaire said that the Chinese philosopher Confucius was the first to articulate a guiding vision without a God. Voltaire and other philosophers of the 'Enlightenment' emulated Confucius, ushered in a new age of science and reason, and brought to an end the age of all-powerful monarchs and their 'divine rights'.

The design and specification of the 'new deal' ordinary people are seeking is beyond the scope of this book and the area of expertise of its author. It's a job for the heirs of the enlightenment philosophers (Newton, Leibniz, Spinoza, Smith, Descartes, Voltaire, Locke, Diderot, Montesquieu, Franklin, Jefferson, Paine, etc.) of the 17th and 18th centuries and of the oriental thinkers who inspired them.

It is clear, however, that the new deal will have to include a new approach to, and philosophy of, business that is less wedded to maximising shareholder value, less hierarchical, better behaved, more ethical and responsive to the needs of employees and societies, fairer in the division of created value and above all, better adapted to the early 21st century business environment.

The new enlightenment philosophers will have to look at the nature of business institutions, at how they're organized, at the hungers that drive them and at the ways in which they are managed. All are 'unfit for purpose' in one way or another.

Two particular problems

The sequence of events that led, over a period of two decades, from the de-regulation of financial services and the shareholder value revolution in the mid-1980s to the financial crisis of 2007–08 and its prolonged recessionary aftermath, exemplifies one of the main problems with management thinking in the second decade of the 21st century; namely that the old law of unintended consequences, first proposed by American sociologist Robert Merton in the 1930s, seems to have extended its rule to almost every management decision.

Most managers want to be decisive, but in recent years too many of their decisions have led them to places they didn't want to go (and could not have foreseen) for them to be sanguine about taking risks and experimenting. The 'no-brainer' decision seems to be going the way of the dodo.

The other problem with modern management thinking is that, although it is obsessed with change and produces enormous numbers of books and articles on 'change management' every year, it still persists in seeing 'change', whether in the business environment or in the organization itself, as something that begins and ends.

Change is transient according to the conventional view. The goal is always to work *through* change towards a new stability.

This assumption is exemplified by the central role still played in management thinking by 'strategy', as the word is normally used.

The company's guiding minds (the CEO and his or her counsellors and advisers) construct a vision of a desired future and draft a plan to arrive there from their point of departure.

The plan proscribes and prescribes. Each action must be consistent with the plan. Profitable opportunities inconsistent with the plan may be rejected and unprofitable opportunities consistent with the plan may be accepted. Course corrections may be needed during the planning period, because things won't always work as hoped. But until things go horribly wrong, the plan will remain the arbiter. Actions will be taken and choices will be made by reference to it.

The strategy, or plan, describes in considerable detail a future in which the leader's 'strategic intent' is realized. This imagined future beckons the organization. If the company strays off course for any reason, it must be nudged back on course. Implementing the plan is the overriding objective, because the company will be deemed to have 'succeeded' only when the leader's strategic intent has finally been realized. This is nirvana, the Promised Land, the new equilibrium, where everyone can take a breath and reflect on a job well done.

But that doesn't seem to work any more, either.

So here we are, in the second decade of the 21st century, wondering where management thinking is going; musing about globalization and the implications of Web 2.0, 3.0, 4.0, etc.; re-packaging old ideas into new platforms such as 'lean'; being frustrated by their apparent loss of effectiveness; looking for the next breakthrough management idea, while doubting whether it will turn out to be anything more than a fad. Management thinking is spinning its wheels; eager to move on, but uncertain about the direction to take, uneasy about choosing the wrong path and struggling to grasp the significance of glitches in the matrix.

We need to re-frame management, to look at it from other angles or through different lenses. Managers could find some answers to the problems that confront them if they abandon their assumptions and conventional wisdoms, put away their strategies and rediscover the original meaning of the Greek word, 'strategus' (see box p. 11).

The pages that follow will look at two unconventional inspirations for the re-invention of western business and its institutions: the military, from which the modern company evolved, and the real live 30-year experiment in business evolution that has been taking place in China.

---

[1] *The Visible Hand: The Managerial Revolution in American Business*: Harvard University Press, 1977.

[2] *The New Rules: How to Succeed in Today's Post-Corporate World*: Free Press, 1995.

[3] Princeton University Press, 1944

[4] *The Selfish Gene:* Oxford University Press, 1976.

[5] *Managing on the Edge: How Successful Companies Use Conflict to Stay Ahead*: Simon & Schuster, 1990.

[6] 'France v Google': *The Economist*, January 12, 2013.

[7] 'What Killed Michael Porter's Monitor Group? The One Force That Really Matters': *Forbes*, November 20, 2012.

[8] 'Strategy and Society: The Link Between Competitive Advantage and Corporate Social Responsibility': *Harvard Business Review*, December, 2006; Creating Shared Value: *Harvard Business Review*, January, 2011.

[9] Jossey-Bass, 2012.

[10] 'How the most innovative companies capitalize on today's rapid-fire strategic challenges – and still make the numbers': *Harvard Business Review*, November 2012.

Chapter 2

Presages

No competition is as intense as full-scale war because in no competition is the end result so momentous for so many people. Defeat is unthinkable in this situation. There is no margin for error and no limit to the resources a nation at war is ready to invest in combat-winning technologies.

That competitors in other areas, including sport and business, see war as the pre-eminent exemplar of all-out competition is evident in the language they use and their interest in the literature of war, and in such authors as von Clausewitz and the Daoist military philosopher, Sun Tszu.

War is more than an analogy. Because it is the most intense, least constrained, most momentous and, in one sense, the purest form of competitive endeavour, military competition blazes the trail that other forms of competition will follow. It is a presage, a leading indicator of where business competition, for instance, is heading. According to this view, the ideas, concepts and technologies that military people are discussing today will be echoed in tomorrow's management discourse.

The message is clear. If business leaders want to get some idea of where business competition is heading, they should look at what the military are up to.

In trying to gain insights for business from contemporary military discussions, it is first necessary to understand how the process of military evolution works.

Arms races

If competition improves the breed as Darwin suggested, it would be surprising if the intensity of military competition did not lead to very rapid evolution in military technology, training, strategy and tactics, both between and during wars.

The term 'arms race' first entered popular usage after World War 2 (WW2) when it was used to describe the rapid, iterative escalation in the nuclear weapon arsenals of the US and the USSR to way past an 'Armageddon point', MAD (Mutually Assured Destruction). But the dialectic is as old as life itself.

It is generated by Darwin's process of natural selection. In their struggles to survive, predators and prey must constantly become fleeter of foot or sharper in tooth and claw. Their senses must become more acute, their bodies larger and stronger, their brains smarter. Each improvement by one has to be matched by the other in an endless evolutionary arms race.

It is the same in war and in business. Competitive advantage today is *sine qua non* tomorrow. It's not enough to get ahead once. You must keep innovating (mutating) to stay ahead, because your rivals are always catching you up and threatening to over-take you.

Paired stirrups in horse-riding are thought to have appeared first in China during the Jin Dynasty (265–420 AD). Their introduction to Europe during the 8th or 9th century changed early medieval warfare radically by greatly improving the effectiveness of cavalry.

Stirrups conferred two advantages. Firstly, they linked, through the rider, the horse's thousand-pound weight and 40 miles-per-hour speed to the end of the knight's lance. Secondly, they allowed riders to stand in the saddle and strike downwards with their swords.

Some suggest that the introduction of stirrups, and the power they gave to mounted armoured knights, led directly to the emergence of feudalism in Carolingian France. Whatever the merits of this still unresolved debate, it is certain that stirrups led directly to the dominance of heavy cavalry in medieval warfare until the adoption of the pike in the 13th century.

The pike was a long, wooden shaft with an iron or steel tip. When opposing armies both used pikes, a length 'arms race' often ensued. Some exceeded 6 metres (22 feet). Flemings used pikes to repel the attacks of French knights at the Battle of the Golden Spurs (also known as the Battle of Courtrai) in 1302. The Scots used pikes at the Battle of Bannockburn in 1314. Both of these battles were seen at the time as astonishing victories by commoners over well-equipped and mounted aristocratic military professionals.

The arms race continued . . . closely-packed pike formations lost their competitive advantage with the advent of archers and crossbow-men, and their effectiveness in warfare was finally ended when portable fire-arms (muskets) arrived on the battlefield.

Much later the pike's military essence re-emerged, in the form of the 'spar torpedo' in naval warfare (see below).

Military arms races are technology-driven competitions and take a characteristic form: constant preparation in peacetime, punctuated by rapid deployment and testing during a war and then, towards the end of the conflict, a period of intense and desperate experimentation. Inter-bellum preparation, with its arms races, is a substitute for war and designed to defer it. 'To avoid War,' said Sun Tszu in *The Art of War*, 'prepare fully for it'.

High technology competitions, such as Formula 1 motor racing, have war-like attributes: intense 'arms race' preparations between each race and each season, punctuated by a series of 'hot wars' at race tracks.

End-of-war experiments, such as the nuclear bombs and rockets at the end of WW2, presage the technologies and the strategic ideas associated with them that will come to dominate the initial stages of the next war.

And, as in nature, the dynamics of arms races mean that from small beginnings great weapons and weapon systems can grow.

Naval warfare

A new chapter in the long history of naval warfare opened in the United States on March 8, 1862 when the Confederate warship *C.S.S. Virginia*, better known as the *Merrimack*, the salvaged Union warship on the hull of which had been built a sloping-sided iron-plated superstructure, steamed down the Elizabeth River into Hampton Roads to attack the Union's blockade fleet. After ramming and sinking the 24-gun wooden steam-sailing sloop the *Cumberland*, the *Merrimack* turned her attention to the 50-gun frigate, the *Congress*. An awed Union naval officer watched the strange-looking *Merrimack* fire 'shot and shell into her [*Congress*] with terrific effect while the shot from the *Congress* glanced from her iron-plated, sloping sides without doing any apparent injury'.

Leaving the millennia-old idea of wooden warships in splinters, the *Merrimack* withdrew upriver for the night. Re-armed and re-fuelled, she returned the following morning to complete the destruction of the Union fleet. Her way was barred by an even odder-looking ship; smaller, lower in the water, with one large swivelling gun turret. This was the *U.S.S. Monitor*, also clad in iron. She lacked the *Merrimack's* armament, but she was more agile, harder to hit and her guns had a 360 degree field of fire.

The crews of the blockade fleet stood on the decks of their wooden ships and watched in amazement as these alien vessels blasted away at each other. The encounter was inconclusive. Although completely different in design and concept, the *Monitor* and the *Merrimack* were well-matched. Neither inflicted serious damage on the other. The lesson both sides took away from the encounter was that, in the new age of ironclad warships, they needed better guns.

The moral victory was the *Monitor's*, because she had saved the Union's fleet from annihilation. But although the wooden fleet survived to fight another day, the wooden warship was clearly doomed.

As often happens after the arrival of disruptive technology, there followed a period of intense chaotic experimentation in the design and specifications of ironclads as naval architects and tacticians sought the best combination of speed, manoeuvrability, armour and armament. In the mid-1880s, something approaching a standard design emerged in the form of the *Majestic* class of battleship, after the British ship of that name. Made of steel and hardened steel armour, *Majestic* class battleships were armed with main batteries of heavy guns and secondary batteries of lighter weapons. They were powered by coal-fuelled triple-expansion steam engines.

Majestic battleships were subsequently built all over the world. They comprised the bulk of both the Russian and Japanese fleets during the Battle of Tsushima on May 27, 1905, 40 years after the end of the American Civil War.

The following year the game changed again with the launch of a new British battleship, *H.M.S. Dreadnought*. It was larger, faster (powered by steam turbines) and had 'all-big-gun' armament (12- and 13-inch). This set the new standard for capital ships. The Dreadnought-building arms race between Britain and Germany was a prelude to World War 1 (WW1). The basic design, subsequently developed and refined with the addition of new armament, such as anti-aircraft guns, remained more or less unchanged until the 1950s, when the battleship ceded its position as the capital ship to the aircraft carrier.

From *Merrimack* to *Dreadnought* in 43 years.

Another Civil War presage of the future for naval warfare occurred on the evening of February 17, 1864, barely a year after the epic encounter between the *Merrimack* and the *Monitor*. The Confederacy's *H. L. Hunley* (also known as *Fish Boat*) sank the Union's 1,200-ton screw sloop *U.S.S. Housatonic* in Charleston harbour and became the first 'submarine' to sink an enemy ship, a feat not repeated until WW1. The *Hunley* - named after its inventor, Horace Lawson Hunley - was powered by a hand-cranked propeller and was armed with a 'spar torpedo', a bomb fixed to the end of a long pole, or spar.

Half a century later, on September 22, 1914, the German submarine U-9, armed with self-propelled torpedoes fuelled with compressed air, sank three British cruisers in less than hour.

The first design for a submarine-launched ballistic missile system (SLBM) was designed by German engineers at the end of WW2. The war ended before it was tested, but the engineers who had worked on it went on to work for the US and Soviet SLBM programmes. Early SLBM systems required a submarine to be surfaced when firing a missile but, on July 20, 1960, the US made the first successful underwater launch of a *Polaris A1* missile. It was a race and the Soviets were snapping at Uncle Sam's heels: the USSR made its first successful underwater launch of a ballistic missile 40 days later.

From the Hunley, with its spar torpedo, to Polaris in 96 years.

Merrimack to *Dreadnought*; *Hunley* to *Polaris*; a land version of the iron-clad known as the 'Land ship', and the Gotha bomber of WW1, to the modern battle tank and the stealth bomber. Visionaries, such as Horace

Hunley, John Ericsson, the designer of the *Monitor*, Colonel Jean Baptiste Estienne, who declared in August 1914, '*La victoire appartiendra, dans cette guerre, à celui des deux belligérants qui parviendra le premier à placer un canon de 75mm sur une voiture capable de se mouvoir en tout terrain*' ('Victory will go, in this war, to the one of the two belligerents who will be the first to succeed in mounting a 75mm gun on a vehicle capable of moving in all types of terrain'), and Wernher von Braun, designer of the WW2 V2 rocket, sometimes see where each arms race is heading.

Robert Oppenheimer, father of the atom bomb, feared where the arms race he started might lead. After the first successful test in New Mexico in July 1945, he quoted Vishnu in the *Bhagavad Gita*: 'Now I am become Death, the destroyer of worlds.'

The privations caused by wars also help to determine the direction of technological advance.

In WW2, German chemists manufactured synthetic oil and oil products with the Bergius process, using coal as the feedstock. The Bergius plants became Germany's main source of aviation fuel and synthetic oil, rubber, methanol and ammonia. By early 1944, German synthetic oil production exceeded 124,000 barrels a day. The Fischer–Tropsch process was also used in wartime Germany and was brought to the US after the war. A 7,000 barrel-a-day plant was built at Brownsville in Texas. It operated from 1950 to 1955, but became uneconomic and was closed when huge new oil discoveries in the Middle East caused the price of oil to plummet.

There were other presages of future warfare in WW2. The German V1 pulse-jet flying bomb heralded cruise missiles and other precision-guided munitions and the switch from 'ready-aim-fire', to 'ready-fire-aim'. Jet and rocket engines made their appearance at the end of the war. Radar, and breaking the German Navy's Enigma Code with machines that evolved into computers, foreshadowed the modern quest for 'information superiority'.

The military's insatiable hunger for information is evident in the enormous resources it devotes to all types of communications, surveillance and espionage. These investments have also helped to shape the modern civilian world. The Internet, for example, emerged from ARPANET, a

Cold War 'packet-switched' communications network developed by the US Defense Department's Advanced Research Projects Agency in 1963.

The first satellite navigation system, *Transit*, was developed for the US Navy. In 1973, a top-level meeting at the Pentagon approved the creation of a Defense Navigation Satellite System (DNSS). The satellites were christened *Navstar*, and the whole system was known as *Navstar-GPS*, later shortened to *GPS*.

But while focused on its own intense and well-funded arms race, the military gives to business more than technological infrastructure. The evolution of military thinking about tactics, strategy, the nature of its environment and its enemies can also inform business thinking.

Presages of business competition

The visionaries who see where the arms race is going discuss with one another the future of warfare. The resource allocations that result from such discussions are self-fulfilling in the sense that they help to determine the direction of the arms race.

Most of these discussions are secret, of course, but some hints can be deduced from military resource allocations. If, as suggested at the start of this chapter, military competition is blazing a trail other forms of competition will follow, these resource allocations may give an indication of where business competition is going.

In recent years, three military stratagems have come to prominence and can be said to characterize modern warfare.

Unmanned

Unmanned Air Vehicles (UAVs), or 'drones,' have been used by the military for almost as long as manned aircraft. In WW1 the British Army's Royal Flying Corps, which later became the Royal Air Force (RAF), used them as targets for gunnery practice. Drones have been listed in *Jane's All the World's Aircraft* since the 1920s.

The US Air Force (USAF) used drones for reconnaissance in the Korean War and as 'special purpose aircraft' in the Vietnam War. Towards the end of the Vietnamese conflict, there were plans to widen the role of UAVs beyond reconnaissance to 'air defense suppression' (knocking out radar installations and anti-aircraft batteries) and there was even talk of using 'combat' UAVs for front-line strike missions.

When manned, tactical reconnaissance planes operated from aircraft carriers became badly over-stretched in the Gulf War, interest in UAVs revived. They proved very useful in Operation Desert Storm as tactical intelligence gatherers and were also used by UN and NATO peacekeepers in the former Yugoslavia.

In the 1990s, the US DoD's *Joint Vision 2010* report emphasized the crucial importance of 'Information Superiority' and saw a role for UAVs in achieving it. The USAF *New World Vistas* report considered missions for UAVs other than reconnaissance and suggested smaller UAVs (Micro Air Vehicles, MAVs) might also have a role to play.

In the campaign against al-Qaeda and the Taliban, the RQ-1 Predator UAV attracted a lot of media coverage. Eight metres long, with a wingspan of 15 metres, it had a drooping, inverted V tail, pusher prop, and a bulbous nose for sensors. In its original version there was nothing 'predatory' about the Predator. It was unarmed and had a maximum speed of only 140mph. It could cruise at 25,000 feet, however, had a range of 450 miles and could stay on station for 16 hours.

The device began to live up to its name in the General Atomics MQ-1 Predator, armed with Hellfire air-to-ground missiles. An armed UAV is known as an 'unmanned combat air vehicle' (UCAV). MQ-1s were first deployed in late 2001 from bases in Pakistan and Uzbekistan. Most were used for assassinating terrorist leaders in Afghanistan. Since then, there have also been reported cases of such attacks in Pakistan, Yemen and Somalia by MQ-1 Predators and other UCAVs such as the Reaper.

The expansion of UAV missions from intelligence, surveillance and reconnaissance to electronic attacks, strike missions, the suppression of air defences, network node or communications relays and search and rescue, for instance, was accompanied by a substantial increase in their deployment under the Obama administration.

Targeted assassinations were authorized by the Bush administration one week after the 9/11 terrorist atrocities in 2001. Over the next seven years, the administration is thought to have ordered about 50 armed drone attacks. President Obama is thought to have sanctioned more than 350 in his first four-year term.[1]

Not surprisingly, the UAV arms race has driven rapid technological development. Today's UAVs combine remote control with computerized automation. Some have on-board systems that can perform low-level human pilot duties such as speed and flight-path stabilization and simple navigation functions, such as way-point following. UAVs are on an evolutionary path that is leading towards more 'autonomy' so that they can make more decisions without human intervention.

Autonomy technology is still in its infancy, but is progressing on several fronts. One area of particular interest to researchers is systems that can combine information gathered by the latest UAVs' proliferating array of electromagnetic, gamma ray, biological and chemical sensors. The aim of all the development effort is to make UAVs smarter and, by adding ever more functionality, eventually to dispense altogether with a human controller. It remains to be seen whether these 'bottom-up' efforts to make UAVs 'smarter' will lead UAV researchers into areas being explored in the 'top-down' search for 'artificial intelligence' (see p. 81).

An extension of 'unmanned' warfare from air to sea was revealed in October 2012, when the US Navy announced that it had fired armour-piercing Spike missiles from a moving remote-controlled inflatable boat and had hit a floating target two miles away. Mark Moses, the Navy's program manager for the armed drone boat project, said that the tests were a 'significant step forward in weaponizing surface unmanned combat capability'. The Navy is calling the 11-metre boat armed with a dual-pod launcher a 'Precision Engagement Module'. It could be used for coastal defence, anti-pirate missions in Somali waters, and merchant vessel protection in high-risk waterways, such as the Straits of Hormuz.[2]

The attraction of UAVs and their marine equivalents for President Obama is clear. Insofar as they undertake missions that previously could only have been undertaken by manned aircraft, they remove human pilots and navy personnel from harm's way. There's a significant cost advantage too. The price tag of the next generation F35 fighter is expected to be $130m. An armed Reaper costs $53m. Drones exemplify the Obama philosophy: clinical strikes, minimum loss of life, low cost.

'Shock and awe' is yesterday's battle cry; today's military victors whisper. They want to tread as lightly as possible.

The fifth domain

Information superiority, clinical strikes, no loss of life: what's not to like about cyber warfare for warriors who want to leave the lightest possible footprints?

It is a furtive, secret war, fought out far below the threshold of public awareness. But there is no doubt about the seriousness with which the Obama administration takes it. William J. Lynn, Obama's Deputy Secretary of Defense, has said that, 'as a doctrinal matter, the Pentagon has formally recognized cyberspace as a new domain in warfare . . . just as critical to military operations as land, sea, air and space'.

Soon after his inauguration in 2009, President Obama said America's digital infrastructure was a 'strategic national asset' that had to be protected. A year later, in May 2010, the Pentagon launched U.S. Cyber Command (USCYBERCOM), led by General Keith Alexander, director of the National Security Agency. Similarly, the UK has established a cyber-security and operations centre at Government Communications Headquarters (GCHQ) and the European Union has set up the European Network and Information Security Agency (ENISA).

The flurry of institution-building for waging what the influential *The Economist* magazine has called 'War in the fifth domain'[3] is the culmination of a growing unease about the vulnerability of our public and private facilities, banking and finance, transport, manufacturing, medical, education and government, to cyber threats and so-called 'logic bombs'.

In the military domain, the potential for cyber espionage has long been recognized. 'Traditional human spies risk arrest or execution by trying to smuggle out copies of documents' *The Economist* noted, but '. . . those in the cyberworld face no such risks'. The article quoted a 'senior American military source' as saying: 'A spy might once have been able to take out a few books' worth of material. Now they take the whole library. And if you re-stock the shelves, they will steal it again.'

Cyber security, including counter-intelligence and defence against logic bombs, is one thing. But there would be no need for cyber defence if you were not – or you couldn't be – sure you would not come under attack in cyberspace. And isn't attack always said to be the best form of defence? It is hard to tell how much cyber-attacking goes on, but the name has emerged from the cloud of one particular dimly perceived but allegedly formidable cyber warrior: Stuxnet.

Stuxnet is a sophisticated computer worm. Discovered in June 2010, it spreads through Microsoft Windows, but is extremely fussy about what it attacks. It is interested only in one particular piece of software on a particular make of computer: the supervisory control and data acquisition systems of Siemens computers that control and monitor particular industrial processes.

Nothing has ever been formally acknowledged and no organization or nation has claimed responsibility. But it's known that most of the computers infected by Stuxnet worldwide were in Iran and that Iran is using secretly procured Siemens computers, covered by the trade sanctions against the country, in its nuclear programme. It is now widely believed that the intended target of the Stuxnet attack was Iran's Natanz uranium enrichment plant.

So who did it?

Experts have found some clues in the weapon itself.

Unlike most 'malware', Stuxnet doesn't harm computers and networks that do not meet its target specifications. The worm spreads fast, but remains quiescent unless it detects Siemens software. And it's time-limited: it was programmed to self-destruct on June 24, 2012.

Stuxnet is also unusually large at half a megabyte and is written in several different programming languages, which is also uncommon.

The worm's extraordinary sophistication, and the enormous lengths to which its creators went to confine its attack to its specified target, have led some experts to conclude that Stuxnet required the most expensive development effort in malware history. Many believe that only a nation-state would have had the necessary resources to create Stuxnet.

Which nation-state?

Israel and the US, possibly both working together, are reckoned to be the most likely culprits.

In the event, Stuxnet isn't thought to have inflicted any permanent damage on the Natanz plant. But, like the *Merrimack* ironclad, it's the first of its kind. It took 43 years to get from the *Merrimack* to the *Dreadnought*. 'Arms race' evolution in cyberwarfare proceeds at a far faster pace than evolution in naval warfare. Imagine what Stuxnet's progeny could be capable of in a few years.

On September 1, 2011, a new worm was found thought to be related to Stuxnet. It was christened 'Duqu' and is thought to be designed to capture keystrokes and system information, possibly in preparation for a future Stuxnet-like attack. In May 2012, a second derivative of Stuxnet called 'Flame' was found, designed to propagate infection through USB drives. A third variant, called 'Gauss', targeted at the banking sector has also emerged, and a new variant of Flame, called 'Mini-Flame', was found in October 2012. Mini-Flame may represent a new generation of cyber weapons.

According to Eugene Kaspersky, a leading expert on cyber wars: 'If Flame and Gauss were massive cyber-espionage operations infecting thousands of users, then Mini-Flame is a high-precision, surgical attack tool.' At a conference in Dubai, Kaspersky predicted that in 2013 there would be an 'escalation of cyber weapons'.

Experts were awed by the size of the investment in Stuxnet. It has been estimated that, quite apart from designing and specifying the weapon, simply writing the code would have taken many months, if not years. The group developing Stuxnet is thought to have been up to 30 strong: hence, the conviction that a nation-state had to be behind it. But for a nation-state, this investment was chicken-feed compared to the time and resources required to develop a new physical weapon system.

Visions of futures made conceivable by modern technology sometimes appear first in science-fiction books and films. In this case, the fourth in the *Die Hard* series of films starring Bruce Willis (*Live Free or Die Hard*, 2007) relates how the hero, John McClane, joins up with a computer hacker, Matt Farrell, to frustrate a cyber attack on America's computer-controlled infrastructure systems.

There's also a worry that the way software systems evolve through the accumulation of standard software 'objects' that may have been written decades ago, before the threat of cyber attack was real or realized, makes them particularly vulnerable to attack.

Special operations

The origins of special forces lie in the British gentleman warrior tradition, as exemplified by James Bond, during the colonial era. One of these Victorian imperial heroes, James Abbott, has a particular resonance in the modern era because he gave his name to a town in Pakistan, Abbottabad, where Osama bin Laden was killed.

Special forces (small, highly trained, well-equipped teams sent on unconventional, high-risk missions) became an important component of modern warfare during WW2 when Britain's Prime Minister Winston Churchill called for 'specially trained troops of the hunter class who can develop a reign of terror down the enemy coast'. The first such unit was the British 'Commandos', formed in 1940. They went on to spawn other specialist units, including the Parachute Regiment, the Special Air Service (SAS), the Special Boat Service, the Long Range Desert Group who served in North Africa, and the Chindits, teams of commandos and Gurkhas who operated from bases deep behind Japanese lines in the Burma Campaign.

The American Charlie Beckwith was attached to the SAS when serving in Vietnam. He was impressed and urged the Pentagon to establish similar units. His advocacy eventually bore fruit in the late 1970s with the formation of Delta Force, and soon afterwards the Sea Air Land (SEAL) teams.

As Robert Fry, Deputy Commanding General of the coalition's forces in Iraq for most of 2006, has pointed out, before 9/11, 'America's strategic world view was dominated by the Powell doctrine ... which resolved only to deploy US forces under conditions of overwhelming superiority'.[4] This was Sun Tszu's prescription in *The Art of War*, a book much admired by Colin Powell. Donald Rumsfeld, US Secretary of Defense from 2001 to 2006, saw this doctrine as a licence for profligate military spending, and favoured the use of special forces instead. The strategy worked well initially in Afghanistan, but not so well in Iraq, where a 'surge' of conventional forces was deemed necessary before disengagement.

Fry says a new US counter-terrorist doctrine is emerging; 'killing the bad guys, at as great a distance as possible. It is punitive rather than conciliatory, and has the decisive advantage of being cheap. 'Why', asked Vice President Joe Biden, '. . . put US boots on the ground when the occasional special forces raid . . . can do the same job without hazard to American life . . .?'.

But the driving force behind the new counter-terrorist strategy is President Obama himself, and there is no doubt that he has taken significant military, diplomatic and political risks in supporting the use of special forces in general, and in sanctioning Operation Neptune Spear, the raid on bin Laden's compound in Abbottabad, in particular. It could have gone badly wrong, as did Operation Eagle Claw in April 1980, when an attempt to rescue American hostages in Iran ended in humiliating failure.

More than an analogy

Business is not war. All may be fair in love and war, but that's not so in business. There are more rules, codes, regulations and laws for business than for war and the penalties for violating and flouting them are much greater. Business isn't an all-out attack on markets that, once conquered, remain fiefdoms until stronger, better-armed businesses conquer the conquerors.

No blood is spilt in business. There are no bombs or bullets. It's an essentially pacific pursuit of value, a creative, rather than a destructive, enterprise. A positive-sum game.

But similarities and correspondences between war and business have long been recognized. The language of business management is still littered with military roots and references. The 'business as war' tradition (exemplified by Dick Fuld, former CEO of Lehman Bothers, who is said to have referred to the investment bank's competitors as 'enemies' whose throats must be 'ripped out', and to have urged employees to act as though they were 'at war'), is out of fashion now, but Sun Tszu's *The Art of War* remains an important management text.

The similarities between business and the military during times of both war and peace are more than skin-deep. For one thing, the key competitive dimensions are the same in both kinds of competition: the quantity of available economic resources; the quality of human resources; scientific and technological innovation; the ability to gather, analyse and interpret information. The domains of war and business also share a dialectical dynamic known as the 'arms race' that impels the protagonists to strive constantly for a decisive edge, a competitive advantage, over their competitors. In business as in war many battles may be won or lost before the final outcome is decided. In both domains, the dialectic is essentially Darwinian – business and military institutions evolve through the selection of beneficial attributes or competitive edges.

Edges take many forms: technological leads; fitter, better trained and more committed and determined personnel; superior intelligence systems and conceptual platforms; better adaptations to the domain environment; more resources of all kinds, particularly money, and more organizational power.

Some edges are more durable than others, but, as a general rule, it is fair to say that today's 'differentiation criterion' (edge) is tomorrow's 'qualification criterion' (commodity). On March 8 1862, the Confederate navy had an edge in the American Civil War, in the form of the *Merrimack*. It sank the 24-gun *Cumberland* and destroyed the 50-gun *Congress*. The following day the edge became a commodity when the Union's *Monitor* steamed into Hampton Roads.

But, as already noted, war is not business.

It wouldn't do for a company to develop an armed drone to take out a rival's manufacturing facility, to drop 'logic bombs' on its ERP system, or to hire a professional assassin to kill its CEO.

There are business equivalents of drones, cyber weapons and special forces, however – adaptations of President Obama's three favoured modes of warfare to the business domain. Before examining them in Chapter 5, we will look in Chapter 3 at the characteristics of the environment that has made these stratagems so attractive to the US President, and in Chapter 4 at a business culture – China's – that it evolving within it.

---

[1] 'Undeclared and Undiscussed': *Financial Times*, October 22, 2012.

[2] *Wired*: Danger Room. October 26, 2012.

[3] July 1 2010.

[4] 'Survival of the fittest': *Prospect*, November 2012.

A new environment

The Obama administration's use of drones, cyber weapons and special forces represented a clear break with Colin Powell's doctrine of 'shock and awe'. The groundwork was laid by Donald Rumsfeld during his second term as US Secretary of Defense from 2001 to 2006 under President George W. Bush (he had previously served as in the same post from 1975 to 1977 under President Gerald Ford). But it was under Obama that the three components acquired the status of a new military doctrine.

Why was a new doctrine of war necessary? To what problem or set of problems were drones etc part of the solution?

Robert Gates, Rumsfeld's successor as Secretary of Defense who had remained in post with bipartisan support after Obama's arrival at the White House, was not a fan of shock and awe. After he retired in 2011 (he was replaced by CIA director Leon Panetta), the former Senator David Boren said Gates would, 'be remembered for making us aware of the danger of over-reliance on military intervention as an instrument of American foreign policy'. The 'big stick' was out of favour. It wasn't just too expensive, it was inappropriate.

The origins of this disenchantment with the Powell doctrine can be traced back to the mid-1990s and to ideas being discussed at that time at the US Army War College in Carlisle, Pennsylvania. In an article in *Fortune*, Lee Smith reported that Carlisle students, the US Army's generals-in-waiting, were 'told time and again that they are preparing for leadership roles in a world that is violent, uncertain, complex, and ambiguous. They hear it so often they have taken to calling the place . . . VUCA U'.[1]

It's not clear whether Smith misheard, or whether the acronym was subsequently re-crafted, but these days the 'V' in VUCA stands for 'volatile', rather than 'violent'. The acronym is sometimes given a final 'D', as in VUCAD, standing for the 'delay' between receipt of raw data, and the emergence of its meaning. Some have suggested that the 'D' should stand for 'deception'.

But VUCA is the standard description of the modern decision-making environment of the US military:

- **V = Volatility**
- **U = Uncertainty**
- **C = Complexity**
- **A = Ambiguity**

Volatility: uncontrollable events (such as financial crises, political and social upheaval, natural catastrophes) occur more frequently than in the past, and prices gyrate more wildly. It's not uncommon these days for stock markets to move more than 2% per day.

Uncertainty: growing event density and volatility make it very hard to predict the future. This undermines the authority of even the most respected forecasters, and makes it possible for two acknowledged 'experts' to derive diametrically opposed conclusions from the same set of data.

Complexity: in the modern world, with its interconnected economies and supply chains and increasingly communicative societies, it has become harder to connect causes to effects. It will become harder still in future, because of the mind-boggling rate at which we are generating new data (see box below).

Ambiguity: the confusion of causes and effects makes its harder to divine the significance or implications of particular events or to know who are your allies and who are your enemies (witness the so-called 'green-on-blue' attacks by supposed 'allies' on Nato soldiers in Afghanistan).

Yottadata

According to Yahoo, there was one day in the summer of 2010 when we produced more data than we had generated since the dawn of human history up to that day. We are producing so much data now that we're running out of words to describe it.

In 1991, the General Conference on Weights and Measures met to add prefixes to the metric system, to handle very large and very small scales of measurement.

We're all familiar with the 'terabyte', a trillion, 10 followed by 12 noughts. The 'peta' (as in 'petabyte'), a quadrillion; 10 with 15 noughts, has started to crop up here, and there. The 'exabyte', a quintillion, 10 with 18 noughts, has made an appearance. In its forecasts of annual global Internet Protocol (IP) traffic in 2016, Cisco talked of the 'zettabyte', a sextillion, 10 with 21 noughts. That's almost as far as the 1991 General Conference on Weights and Measures felt it necessary to go.

Next and last in the numerological lexicon, as large as Conference delegates felt it necessary to go, was the 'yotta', a septillion, 10 with 24 noughts. The diameter of the observable universe is 880 'yottameters'. Andrew McAfee, principal research scientist at the MIT Center for Digital Business, estimates that the annual volume of digital traffic will be in the 'yottabyte' region by the end of this decade.

The sciences of complexity

The emphasis placed on VUCA by those Army War College teachers may have been inspired by James Gleick's book, *Chaos*, which was short-listed for a Pulitzer Prize in 1988.[2]

Chaos introduced the world to a hitherto obscure branch of science and mathematics known as the sciences of complexity and to the so-called 'butterfly effect', first described in the 1960s by Edward Lorenz, and named after the title of a talk he gave in 1972 to the American Association for the Advancement of Science: *Does the flap of a butterfly's wings in Brazil set off a tornado in Texas?*

Complexity scientists study the behaviour of 'non-linear' systems.

To say a system is 'complex' is very different from saying that it is 'complicated.' An extremely complicated system is 'linear': its chains of causes and effects are fixed, and thus predictable. But a complex system is non-linear; there is no definable logic path linking a cause to an effect. There is a unique solution to a 'complicated' problem. Since there may be several or no solutions to a complex problem it is inherently insoluble.

A linear system can be understood and controlled by understanding and controlling all of its sub-systems. But a non-linear system is 'synergistic'; it has qualities and behaves in ways that cannot be understood and controlled in a similar way.

The 'C' in VUCA means that the VUCA world is populated by 'Complex Adaptive Systems', also known as 'non-linear feedback systems'. A distinctive characteristic of such systems, the butterfly effect, is that they are extremely sensitive to initial conditions. Small, undetectable shocks can, and often do, lead to fundamental changes in the behaviour of the whole system.

Lorenz discovered this surprising result by accident, when using a computer model to rerun a weather prediction in 1961. To save time he entered one variable as 0.506, instead of the full 0.506127. He saw a completely different weather pattern emerge.

This is the VUCA world – a world where a decision by an apocryphal young home-owner in Cleveland, Ohio to spend his wages on a ticket for the ballgame instead of paying his mortgage can bring, through a sequence of events that no-one could have predicted, the world's banking system to its knees; a world where the harassment by local officials of a market trader in Tunisia can lead, via a sequence of events no one could have predicted, to revolts and revolutions and a re-writing of the political map of North Africa and parts of the Middle East.

VUCA is the law of unintended consequences writ global.

It has been strongly corroborated for the US military by the messy and unpredicted aftermaths of the 'shock and awe' interventions in Iraq and Afghanistan. After the fall of Saddam, Iraq seemed to be the prisoner of the coalition's army. It soon became apparent that the boot was on the other foot.

The reason why the Obama administration prefers to tread much more lightly is that, although they can't predict the consequences of a drone strike, a cyber attack or a special forces mission, they can be reasonably confident that, even in a VUCA world, the more lightly you tread, the fewer and less dramatic the unintended consequences.

Unpredicted events with unpredictable consequences are becoming an important characteristic of our times – the new *zeitgeist*. Nature seems to be joining in. At the time of writing, hurricane Sandy is battering America's eastern seaboard. Devastating floods, volcanic eruptions, earthquakes and tsunamis are commonplace. Nowadays the eponymous hero of Shakespeare's *King Lear* could easily be mistaken for a television news or weather presenter:

> *Blow, winds, and crack your cheeks! rage! blow!*
> *You cataracts and hurricanoes, spout*
> *Till you have drench'd our steeples, drown'd the cocks!*
> *You sulphurous and thought-executing fires,*
> *Vaunt-couriers to oak-cleaving thunderbolts,*
> *Singe my white head! And thou, all shaking thunder,*
> *Strike flat the thick rotundity o' the world!*

Instant communication through the global cloud has not created the VUCA world, but, by accelerating the speed at which effects follow causes, responses follow stimuli and consequences follow actions, and multiplying the connections between agents, it has stimulated the activity within and enhanced the self-organizing properties of the complex adaptive systems that comprise the VUCA world.

The vocal majority

Having conquered distance (to live at the back-of-beyond or in the boondocks is no disadvantage now), the gale of creative destruction that is the Internet ended conjecture (if you don't know or can't remember, there's no need to speculate or rack your brains any more) and has turned its lethal attention to the 'silent majority'. We no longer have to suffer in silence or mutely accept the decisions and dispositions of others.

People find their own uses for technology, and they have chosen to use the Internet and its hand-held terminal, the 'smart phone', to speak and show, through a proliferating variety of platforms: websites,

YouTube, Facebook, Twitter, blogs and microblogs, and other so-called 'social media' yet to be devised.

Wikipedia has revealed another human propensity, the existence of which was unsuspected before the advent of the Internet: people want to share what they know and will do so for free, given half a chance. By January 2013, the English-language Wikipedia (there are many others) had accumulated more than 4.1 million articles, equivalent to a traditional encyclopaedia of over 1,700 volumes.

This is an achievement by the people, for the people. There was no directing mind after Jimmy Wales and Larry Sanger had launched the system. A combination of the idea, the Internet and Wiki software triggered a global orgy of knowledge sharing. The system is extremely democratic. Wiki software allowing on-site editing exemplifies that ethos. (Some say 'Wiki' stands for 'What I Know Is', but that is a so-called 'backronym'. The word is Hawaiian for 'fast'.)

It will be suggested, in Chapter 6, that the fact that this vast body of knowledge has been accumulated for free, without any payments at all to contributors, has important implications for the future of business transaction costs.

Wikipedia apart, most of what is written and shown on the vast open space of the Internet is banal, prosaic, parochial, trivial, weird or silly. A great deal of it is inaccurate, untrue or wrong. Much is pornographic. Some of it is dangerous, criminal or subversive. But within all the junk in the untold trillions of bits being uploaded and downloaded each second there are revelations, exhortations and arguments that move hundreds, thousands, and sometimes millions of people to act in commercially or politically significant ways.

This, more than any other quality, differentiates the modern world from the past. It is still early days. People are still exploring possibilities, and experimenting. But some of the significance of this end of silence for business and political leaders is becoming apparent.

Losing control

Communications have always played a vital role in gathering support for uprisings and revolutions. The Protestant reformer, Martin Luther, used printed posters to good effect in his struggles against the papacy in the early 16th century. The American revolutionary, Thomas Paine, used pamphlets or libels (from the Latin 'libellus', meaning a little book) in the late 18th century, including the original bestseller *Common Sense* (1776). Fellow revolutionary, John Adams, said: 'Without the pen of the author of "Common Sense," the sword of Washington would have been raised in vain.'

Two centuries later, the Solidarity movement in Poland spread its message of opposition and, in so doing, heralded the dissolution of the Soviet Union, with the help of smuggled Xerox machines.

Text messaging on mobile phones played a key role in the 2001 EDSA 2 revolution in the Philippines, which led to the overthrow of the President, Joseph Estrada.

Demonstrations against the government of José María Aznar in Spain ahead of the 2004 election, won by José Luis Rodríguez Zapatero's Socialist Party, were said to have been organized by text messages from mobile phones.

Mobile phones and text messages are widely believed to have played a key role in fostering the Orange Revolution in Ukraine in 2005.

A mass protest against the terrorist Revolutionary Armed Forces of Colombia (FARC) occurred in February 2008 in Colombia itself and many other cities around the world, organized through Facebook and Skype (Voice over Internet Protocol) plus text messages on mobile phones.

An allegedly rigged election victory by the ruling Communist Party in Moldova in April 2009 led to mass, Twitter-organized, protests in several cities. This de-stabilized Moldovan politics and led to another election in July 2009. The Communist Party emerged as the largest party, but could not form a government and was replaced by a coalition of opposition parties.

Protests in major cities in Iran following the disputed victory of President Mahmoud Ahmadinejad in the 2009 election were called the Green Revolution, or the Persian Awakening, but also the 'Twitter Revolution', because the protesters used Twitter and other social networking sites to communicate. Most of the information about the protests in Iran came to the West through YouTube and Twitter. A so-called 'viral' video of the death, during the protests, of Neda Agha-Soltan, spread all over the world.

Social media are also said to have played an important part in the Tunisian revolution, which culminated in the fall of President Ben Ali in early 2011. They played a significant role in spreading the news of the suicide that sparked the protests and in multiplying those protests. An estimated 18% of Tunisians were on Facebook and most of those were the educated young who led the protests. Half of Tunisia's television audience watch satellite TV, particularly Al-Jazeera, which is said to have relied heavily on Facebook pages and YouTube reports of events. A new development was the tactical use of Twitter by protesters – there were tweets warning of sniper locations and asking for blood dona-tions, as well those organizing the protests.

Extensive Internet coverage of Tunisia's revolution and references to its precursors in Moldova and Iran helped to prepare the ground for the revolutions and revolts in Egypt, Libya and Syria. And all the while, Facebook, YouTube, Twitter, and television have combined in ever more sophisticated ways.

Combinations of new 'narrowcast' social and traditional broadcast media via satellite, rather than Twitter or Facebook on their own, have proved powerful catalysts for turning latent discontent into civil unrest and rebellion all over the world. As Jared Cohen, of the US State Department's policy planning staff, told *The New York Times* (July 18, 2010). 'The 21st century is a really terrible time to be a control freak.'

In *The Net Delusion*, Evgeny Morozov, a Belarusian-born writer based in the US, takes issue with the 'cyber-utopianism' view. He argues that authoritarian regimes have proved able and willing to curtail and block online access, close websites, and use the social media to infiltrate protest groups, track down troublemakers and promote their own propaganda online.[3]

Morozov has a point. New social media, combined with the old, have not left authoritarianism defenceless against a bottom-up tsunami of protests and rebellion. Commercial Web analysis tools developed mostly in the West provide police states and tyrants with a facility to investigate and analyze trends, identify activists and pre-empt subversion that their Cold-War predecessors would have envied.

But when all is said and done, and when all the costs and benefits for both parties are audited, it is hard not to see the new media as giving more power to the people than to those who would control them. And in any case, this genie cannot be put back into the lamp from which Web technology has liberated it. Whatever side you are on, whatever view you take, whatever you have to gain or lose, you have to live in a world in which the majority is no longer silent; in which bottom-up forces that could precipitate disruptive events at any time, in any place, are permanent features of the political and business environment.

Politics

Although one can be forgiven for forgetting it at the beginning of the second decade of the 21st century, riots, revolts, rebellions and revolutions are rare political events. Most of the time and in most places, politics are argumentative and often heated, but not violent. Their set piece events occur in parliament buildings, the campaign trail and voting booths, not on the streets.

The role social media played in the election of President Obama in 2008 has been well documented. According to the social media guru J. D. Lasica (www.socialmedia.biz), the 1,800 videos Obama's team posted on YouTube attracted 110 million views, the Obama Facebook Group had over three million fans, the MySpace page had 845,000 friends and the Twitter account had over 130,000 followers. It was the first conspicuously successful use of social media in a major election and is generally thought to have heralded a sea change in political campaigning and fundraising.

The use of social media was a differentiator for the Democrats and Obama in 2008, but, as in business, today's differentiation criteria in politics are tomorrow's qualification criteria. The Republicans were soon up to speed.

It is hard to exaggerate the speed with which the social media are changing politics, or how widely their power to change the game is understood. The learning curve is close to vertical everywhere.

An article in *The Christian Science Monitor* in June 2011 reported that numerous independent candidates for local Peoples' Congresses were using social media to challenge the Chinese Communist Party's traditional monopoly of political offices. Candidate Li Chengpeng told the two million or so followers of his Sina Weibo microblog: 'You will never know the benefit of standing up if you always stay on your knees.'

The bodies chosen between May 2011 and December 2012 are at the lowest level of the Chinese government system and deal with local issues, such as garbage collection and local business regulation. But they are the only elected bodies in China, membership of which is not reserved exclusively for Party members.

This was the first time social media had been widely used in local elections in China and the party is uneasy about where the trend might lead. An editorial in the party newspaper, the *Global Times*, acknowledged that 'Opposition sentiment exists in China' but also warned that Chinese society was not 'mature enough to work out how to treat opposition sentiment, nor to decide whether to allow such sentiment to migrate from the Internet, to the real world, nor how far it should be allowed to play a role in Chinese politics'.

Those who wonder why the world has suddenly acquired the qualities summarized by the VUCA acronym – volatile, uncertain, complex, and ambiguous – might find part of the answer in the social media.

In the past, when the masses, the mob, the majority were silent, it seemed not only possible, but reasonable to see them as the social bedrock, the salt of the earth, the foundations on which countries and communities rested. Preoccupied with subsistence and the concerns of daily life, they were biddable, controllable and fundamentally conservative. They had the power (in theory) to oppose and challenge governments but it was a distributed, dilute power, spread thinly through the population, which coalesced into power formidable enough to challenge the *status quo* only in exceptional circumstances. Because there has, until now, been no routine way to concentrate and organize the latent power of the people, the people have until now been silent, and their silence has been taken by their rulers as consent if not contentment.

Not any more.

The stolid, silent masses have become a sometimes self-orchestrated cacophony of strident voices waving pictures and video, expressing disapproval and indignation, making demands, revealing what some would want to remain hidden, organising protests and revolutions, spreading rumour and exhortation, finding common cause, ganging up and generally making nuisances of themselves.

This has two consequences for decision-makers. The first, and more obvious, is that the people have joined the lobbying game. Policy-making between elections is no longer the preserve of corporate or other vested interests, intra-party squabbles, back-room deals, or set-piece face-offs in parliament.

Ordinary Americans were incensed in July 2011 by the debt ceiling stand-off between President Obama's Democrat administration and a Republican-dominated Congress and gave vent to their anger in the social media. The *Washington Post*'s PostPolitics page reported on July 24, 2011 that under the indelicate hashtag #f***youwashington (he didn't use the asterisks), journalism professor, Jeff Jarvis, had tweeted his anger. His hashtag went 'viral' attracting hundreds of responses an hour. Jarvis explained his tweet in a blog posted the following day. 'It pissed me off. I'd had enough . . . I tweeted: "Hey, Washington a**holes, it's our country, our economy, our money. Stop f***ing with it." Then it exploded . . . [The tweets] restore my faith not in government but in society, in us.'

The second and more important consequence of the vocal majority is that the masses can no longer be seen to the same extent as in the past as the inert foundations of society. These days, they are as much a source of uncertainty, ambiguity, and instability as of stability. No one knows which tweet or blogpost will go viral next. With hyper-active social media, novelty emerges from the bottom-up and the most insignificant of events (a tweet, a text, an email or a blogpost) can have major consequences.

VUCA and business

The revolutions in North Africa and the Middle East and the 2007–08 banking crisis and its protracted economic aftermath, particularly in Europe, were 'Black Swan' events: they came completely 'out of the blue'. And they keep on coming – the Eurozone lurches from one crisis to the next; recessions deepened by austerity budgets cause civil unrest; regulatory changes in the banking sector come thick and fast; poor harvests, industrial action at South African mines and Iranian sanctions lead to volatile commodity prices; ambiguous and inconsistent economic indicators add to the uncertainty; trade disputes and growing protectionism threaten the global market; and the possibility of schisms and secession (in the UK and Spain) and the breakup of the Eurozone is undermining the perceived integrity of the world's largest trading bloc.

The environment for business has changed and as good a way as any to characterize the change is to say the business world has become more Volatile, Uncertain, Complex and Ambiguous.

Crises, and how to respond to them, have been fixtures on business agendas since the onset of the banking crisis in 2007. Stimulus packages, austerity budgets, and sovereign debt problems followed. Before companies could draw breath, the 'Jasmine Revolution' broke out in Tunisia, spread to Egypt, Libya and Syria and caused civil unrest all over the Middle East. In March 2011, a major earthquake off the coast of Japan generated a calamitous tsunami that ruined coastal towns, led to an escape of radioactivity at the Fukushima power station and then prompted much heart-searching, particularly in Germany, about the wisdom of 'low-carbon' energy policies based on nuclear power.

Crisis management is mainstream management now. When all managers can be sure of is that unexpected events will occur frequently and will have unpredictable consequences, they need to make their plans provisional and become nimble.

Businesses need to adapt by dispensing with old ideas, such as the assumption that the task of management is to seek adaptation to an equilibrium. There is no equilibrium. They must learn to live with what one Canadian CEO calls 'unmanageable complexity'.

There is a growing recognition within the business community today that the environment has changed and that managers confront a new set of challenges. In their book, *On Good Management: The Corporate Lifecycle*, Burkhard Schwenker and Mario Müller-Dofel suggest that in the new 'complex' business world (as opposed to one that is simply 'complicated' – see above), 'The validity of our traditional strategy and planning concepts is eroding'.[4] The authors identify four 'if-then' Boolean logic gates:

- *If* trends are not reliable, *then* numbers are of limited use as the basis for planning and decision-making.
- *If* numbers can't help us, *then* we must discard the assumption that every management decision can be quantified.
- *If* the business environment is changing fast, *then* 'short-termism' is appropriate.
- *If* people are unsettled by complexity, *then* trust in the abilities of management is crucial.

Schwenker and Müller-Dofel say employees have a psychological need for a sense of security, symbolized by organization charts. 'Look,' they say to themselves, pointing at the chart, 'There's the little box with my name on it. That's my home. That's where I belong.' In an environment where organizational charts, along with much else in modern companies, are provisional and may have to be changed at short notice, being able to convey a sense of security by some other means is an essential task of leadership (see Chapter 9).

Other management writers who acknowledge the advent of 'VUCA' have advocated organizational changes to help companies handle the new business environment.

Harvard Business School professor, John Kotter, for example, urges companies to graft what he calls 'parallel operating systems' onto their conventional hierarchical organization to help them to 'stay competitive amid constant turbulence and disruption'.[5]

Conventional, hierarchical structures and organizational processes have served companies well until now and are still a good way to run a business on a day-to-day basis, says Kotter. 'What they do not do well,' he says, 'is identify the most important hazards and opportunities early enough, formulate . . . initiatives nimbly enough, and implement them fast enough.' His solution is a parallel operating system for designing and implementing strategy, that uses 'an agile, network-like structure and . . . very different . . . processes'.

He says the idea of 'strategy' – 'a word now used loosely to cover sporadic planning around what businesses to be in, and important policies concerning how to compete in those businesses' – needs to evolve. According to Kotter, strategy should be seen as 'a dynamic force that constantly seeks opportunities, identifies initiatives that will capitalize on them and completes the initiatives swiftly and efficiently.' He thinks of the strategic force as a process of 'searching, doing, learning, and modifying . . .' and the network that he proposes as 'a continuous . . . change function . . . that accelerates momentum and agility because it never stops'.

The 'Strategy Network' (SN) consists entirely of volunteer 'change agents' (Kotter says that 10% of employees, including managers, is plenty and possible). It uses different processes and talks in a different language from the hierarchy, but there's a constant flow of information, people and activities between the network and the hierarchy.

At the centre of the SN there is a 'guiding coalition' (GC) around which orbit 'strategic initiatives', each of which may incorporate several sub initiatives. GC members are selected to represent each of the hierarchy's departments and levels, thereby ensuring the coalition incorporates a broad range of skills. All GC members are equal.

The hierarchy doesn't change, but the SN 'can morph with ease', thereby liberating information from the hierarchy's silos and layers. The hierarchy benefits because all of the 'junk', as Kotter calls it, previously pasted on it for tackling 'strategic initiatives', such as work streams, tiger teams and strategy departments, is shifted to the SN.

The SN is energized by 'accelerators', including creating 'a sense of urgency' round the biggest opportunity in sight and other, more conventional, change management prescriptions, such as promoting a vision and strategy to get 'buy in' and attract SN volunteers, and celebrating visible, significant short-term wins.

Kotter says: 'The 21st century will force us all to evolve toward a fundamentally new form of organization . . . The companies that get there first, because they act NOW will see immediate and long-term success – for shareholders, customers, employees, and themselves.'

It's an interesting proposal, and there is nothing to object to in Kotter's diagnosis of the modern management challenge, or in his re-interpretation of strategy as: 'a dynamic force that constantly seeks opportunities, identifies initiatives . . . and completes the initiatives swiftly and efficiently.'

But Kotter's parallel operating system solution seems more a patch on the conventional hierarchical system than 'a fundamentally new form of organization'. It incorporates none of the recent military adaptations to the VUCA environment, and pays less respect than is due to what Isao Endo calls the organization's 'Gemba Power' (see Chapter 7).

Living in VUCA

VUCA does not simply characterize the military environment. It's a description of the world environment and of its subsets, including the business environment. It's a new and different setting for all competition, including business competition.

As noted in Chapter 2, no competition is as intense, because in no competition is the end result so momentous for so many people as full-scale war. It is all-out, no-holds-barred, no-expense-spared competition. In this sense, war is a purer kind of competition than that encountered in the business world. It is less confined by the legal, political, regulatory, financial, social, psychological, aesthetic, moral and ethical constraints to which business is subject, and less wedded to the conventional wisdoms and the institutional and behavioural legacies of the past.

Because the military is less constrained than business and has had more time and resources, as well as a greater need to think deeply about the future, it recognized the advent of, and began to adapt to, VUCA earlier than business.

What would business be like now if business people had recognized the emergence of the new VUCA world earlier, and if the origins of business had been in the mid-20th rather than the mid-19th century?

---

[1] 'New ideas from the Army (really)': *Fortune*, September 19 1994.

[2] *Chaos: Making a New Science*: Viking Penguin, 1987.

[3] *The Net Delusion: How Not to Liberate the World*: Allen Lane, 2011.

[4] *On Good Management: The Corporate Lifecycle*: BrunoMedia Verlag, 2012.

[5] 'How the most innovative companies capitalize on today's rapid-fire strategic challenges – and still make the numbers': *Harvard Business Review*, November 2012.

Chapter 4

A child of VUCA

If you were planning an experiment designed to establish which kinds of business institutions and management styles would have evolved if business had been born into a VUCA world, you would not, if you could help it, choose to start with China in 1978.

There would be too much inherited baggage for a pure experiment: a 3,000-year-old culture, deeply wounded by the Cultural Revolution, but still vibrant and influential; a recent, disastrous experiment with the collective ownership of land and productive resources; an authoritarian government. All this would drown out or distort any effect a VUCA environment might have on the evolution of a nascent business management tradition.

But since you can't re-wind history, re-set the initial conditions to your liking and play the tape again, a VUCA business experiment as pure and uncompromized as the 'total' military competition in a VUCA world, is unavailable. China in 1978, the year of Deng Xiaoping's 'great opening' to the world, is as close to a pure experiment in the evolution of business in a VUCA world as it is possible to get.

And, as a real-life experiment, it has a lot more going for it than it may seem at first sight. For one thing, the timing was close to perfect.

Deng's business laboratory

It is impossible to say precisely when the VUCA world snapped into existence, but some of the elements and triggers that precipitated the phase transition from pre-VUCA to VUCA were assembling just as Deng was embarking on his business experiment. A year before the 'great opening', for example, the age of the personal computer had dawned with the launch of the so-called '1977 trinity': the Apple II, the Commodore PET 2001 and the Tandy TRS-80. (The IBM PC would be launched four years later, in 1981). And a year after China's 'opening', the Iranian revolution heralded the emergence of Islamic fundamentalism as the most significant geopolitical development of the late 20th century.

Another validating characteristic of Deng's experiment was that it was powered by the pure fuel of entrepreneurial energy. China's economy is still dominated by large, state-owned enterprises, but they're not collectively-owned, and they were not the prime movers of China's rapid industrialization during the past three decades. That accolade must go to the 19 farmers of Xiaogang who broke Mao Zedong's farming laws by dividing communally-owned farmland into household plots and to the entrepreneurs who evaded Mao's legal sanctions on individualism and entrepreneurialism by transforming thousands of communally-owned 'Township and Village Enterprises' (TVEs), created during the Great Leap Forward, into the seeds of an essentially capitalist economy.

The farmers of Xiaogang are folk heroes in China now. None of them could write, so they all signed their illegal contract with thumbprints. One of the clauses in their agreement stipulated that, if any were executed for breaking the collectivization laws, the rest would care for their families.

And nor in Deng's hands was the authoritarian character of China's system of government the impediment to a valid experiment it might have been. On the contrary, it was the authority of Deng that made heroes of the Xiaogang farmers and gave the TVE entrepreneurs free rein. Without Deng's authority and approval, it would have been far harder for China's entrepreneurs to escape from the legal legacies of the dead hand of collectivism.

Although Deng's bottom line was always the survival of the Chinese Communist Party (CCP), as the ruler of China, he was a pragmatist. He was not concerned with how the CCP's hegemony was maintained. 'It doesn't matter if a cat is black or white', he used to say, 'as long as it can catch mice'. Full-blooded economic liberalism was a strange bedfellow for authoritarian one-party politics. Deng chose it because it seemed to him to be the best way to feed the people and so preserve CCP rule.

The American dream

A more serious objection to the claim that Deng's experiment was a valid test of business evolution in a VUCA world was his adoption, as a model for the Chinese commercial sector, of the American way of doing business. To contaminate the experimental data with foreign material, American business and management ideas and principles in this case, would be a classic failure of experimental design.

How can one expect to learn anything useful about the VUCA adapted organization from businesses based on a model that embarked on its own evolutionary journey in the mid-19th century?

It's certainly true that Deng himself was, or at any rate was purported to be, beguiled by the American Dream. 'To get rich is glorious,' he said. It is also true that the American way of doing business was extremely influential in China after 1978 and that many thousands of young Chinese men and women, the so-called 'sea turtles', attended American business schools and later returned home bringing with them American business ideas, models, and principles.

But Deng opened the door to the American way of doing business. He didn't prescribe it. His industrial policy was as 'light touch' as his liberal economic policy – no grand plan and no Chinese version of Japan's Ministry of International Trade and Industry (MITI), an institution created in the 1950s to promote and to protect Japan's domestic industries. Instead, Deng's approach was to liberalize the context for business and unshackle China's long outlawed entrepreneurs. Deng was surprised by the eruption of entrepreneurial activity in the 1980s but he saw it as a positive development that could help to realize his vision of a prosperous China.

'To cross the river, you have to feel the stones,' he used to say.

You can't see the stones, but if you take a step at a time in what appears to be the right direction, you will get across safely. This is the credo of a pragmatic opportunist: when a trend consistent with the guiding vision begins, let it run.

For 30 years after Deng's opening up in 1978, the American model of business appeared to have carried all before it in China. US business jargon issued from every executive's lips in the private and public sectors and western business models, tools, techniques and principles were widely adopted. That the Chinese economy grew rapidly during the period was taken as proof of the superiority of the American style of management.

But the correlation between China's rapid growth of imported theories and processes and the adoption should not be taken to indicate causation. A much more likely explanation of China's economic miracle was the liberation of its ancient entrepreneurial culture after the long suppression under Mao. Many Chinese entrepreneurs and business people adopted American methods because such tools were useful, not because they wanted to emulate the US approach in its entirety.

The watershed

The author has suggested elsewhere that 2008 was a watershed. The banking crisis in the US and Europe, and the global economic slowdown that followed – the kind of 'black swan' events that are only to be expected in a VUCA world – came when China's self-confidence was at its height. The first space walk by a Chinese astronaut, from a Chinese spacecraft, the successful Beijing Olympics and the way the Chinese government handled – and the way the people responded to – the Sichuan earthquake.[1]

The US economic model to which Deng had hitched China's star in 1978 seemed to be coming apart. The American dream, and with it the perceived validity of its management models, were called into question. As is the way in a VUCA world, the consequences of this loss of faith in American management models were complex and ambiguous. But one way to characterize them is to say that they were a shock but also a liberation from an alien business culture that initiated a search by China's entrepreneurs for Chinese roots and cultural substrates.

And as luck would have it there were ideas, principles and beliefs in ancient Chinese culture that are extraordinarily well-suited to the VUCA environment.

Luck and movement

Divination systems (the Tarot, crystal balls, the Oracle at Delphi and the witches in *Macbeth*) have been popular at all times, in all places. That China's *I Ching* divination system, which dates back to the third millennium BC, remains popular in China reflects the fatalism of the Chinese and their recognition of the role fortune plays in the fates of nations, individuals and organizations.

Western managers try to minimize the role of luck in business, not always successfully, as the 2007–08 financial crisis showed, with detailed statistical analysis, probability theory and modern risk management techniques.

Chinese managers are opportunistic and stoical – they are quick to exploit good luck and philosophical about bad luck. This attitude to luck is appropriate in the VUCA world where anything can happen without warning, at any moment.

Fate is fixed in other divination systems. *I Ching* predictions are provisional, because change itself is changeable. You can control change to some extent, if you can divine its nature early enough. Managers must always be alert and scan the environment constantly for weak signals heralding major change.

Change is transient in western business cultures; a process with a beginning and an end. A theme in the Chinese culture, running through the *I Ching*, Daoism and Confucianism, is that change is a constantly flowing stream of events subject to immutable laws that govern all change. In Daoism, these laws are known collectively as the 'Dao', the way. Things are always changing into their opposites, success to failure, disadvantage to advantage, loss to profit.

Nothing stays the same, except the way, the path, the Dao.

Daoism is as old as the *I Ching*, but it is usually associated with Lao Tzu, who is thought to have lived during the warring states period in the fifth or fourth century BC. He is said to be the author of the *Dao de Ching* ('the book of the way'). This urged people to live in accordance with the rhythms of nature.

Sun Tszu applied Daoist teaching to what he called *The Art of War*.

Daoists see strife and dissent as a consequence of striving, which confronts us with obstacles. We should stop striving and 'go with the flow', the 'Dao'. Daoism advocates a search for internal balance through practices and disciplines, such as *tai chi*.

There's a hint of Daoism in the way the Communist Party's policies and decisions are perceived. To most Chinese people, they are like the weather: they can be adapted to, and often exploited (as when, for instance, a property developer makes a killing by buying land after a change in social housing policy is heralded in a speech at the National People's Congress). But they can't be resisted. Going with the flow is the only option.

In a VUCA world, where anything can happen, at any time, and where nothing can be taken for granted, there is much to be said for the Daoist outlook on life.

Order and leadership

Disturbed by the violence of his times in the sixth century BC and by what he saw as a lack of moral compass, Confucius prescribed principles for the good ordering of society. The most important is *li*, meaning ritual, but not the formal sequences of actions that the word denotes in English. In Chinese, it means ethical, morally correct behaviour.

Hierarchy is essential to maintain stability. Servants should obey their masters, subjects should obey their rulers, children should obey their parents and wives should obey their husbands. Hierarchy generates the ideas of *ren* (benevolence), *yi* (propriety), *xiao* (filial piety) and *zhong* (loyalty). The family plays a key role in Confucian thought from the level of parents and children through, by analogy, to the state and its people and to the chief executive and his or her employees.

If people in authority, whether kings, masters, or parents, abused their power, they would be violating the norms of what is right and correct. The principle that rulers are in *loco parentis* to their subjects and must never abuse their power pre-dates Confucius. It is known as the 'Mandate of Heaven' (*dian ming*). Rulers' mandates are conditional. If they misbehave or abuse their power, the people have a right to oppose or, if necessary, depose them.

The group – whether a family, organization or the people at large – as the unit of agency in the Confucian world-view, provides no licence for 'ego-tripping' and self-advancement. Individualism and putting oneself forward is selfish and petty.

These ideas also resonate with the exigencies of management in the VUCA world. In a turbulent, unpredictable environment, a sense of internal order is required to nurture and maintain organizational capabilities, or 'Gemba' (see Chapter 5). But the power hierarchical order confers on a leader must be used with great care, and due consideration of the views of other group members, because it is the group that acts.

To summarize this brief summary of the cultural antecedents of the evolving Chinese management approach:

- *Fatalism, a corresponding recognition of the role of luck, and yet a belief that if change is spotted early, it can be controlled to some extent. Hence the need for constant scanning for weak signals heralding major change.*
- *Everything is changing all the time, but within unchanging natural laws. There is change and there is continuity.*
- *A well-ordered society emerges from morally correct behaviour.*
- *Hierarchy is needed to maintain stability, but the power of rulers is conditional on their good behaviour.*
- *The ruler promulgates the 'Dao' ('way'), which plays a role in the lives of ordinary people, much like the weather.*
- *The group, rather than the individual, is the unit of agency.*

Government

China's system of government is organized along federal lines, just as it was in the imperial era. The central Chinese Communist Party (CCP) in Beijing decides general policy direction, and issues instructions to local state and party institutions.

But it's not as simple as that. China's governance system has been characterized as 'fragmented authoritarianism'. Separate state and party institutions seek a policy consensus, through bargaining and negotiation. When consensus can't be achieved, conflict ensues and each group lobbies for its own policies. More 'fragments', in the form of local institutions, joined the system during the great de-centralization of the

1980s and in 2003 another important interest group was added when CCP membership was opened to private business people.

The party and government, although officially separate, are almost totally fused in practice. Party members hold all the significant official posts, and the education and training of all officials at central and local levels is in the hands of CCP institutions.

Through its ownership and use of the *Xinhua* news agency, *CCTV*, and the *People's Daily*, the government cultivates and guides public opinion, tests new policies and gathers support for new priorities and policies.

The state-owned media are generally trusted by the people because, being state-owned, they have no business axes to grind or partisan politics to promote. They're required reading and viewing for most business people. The most adept at analyzing articles and speeches and deducing changes in 'protocol' rankings from seating positions in pictures, and orders of mention in articles, have a competitive advantage over their rivals.

There are many thousands of incidents of civil unrest each year in China, but the opposition they represent is against municipal and local administrators for perceived violations of property rights, for example, rather than against central government. By and large, the people trust the government, and agree with its priorities and policies.

The five-year plans – the 12th was unveiled in 2011 covering the period 2011 to 2015 – provide a strategic framework for business.

In substituting 'transforming the economic development model', for the previous 'transforming the economic growth model' the new plan switched the focus from the quantity, to the quality of growth. It is comprehensive, detailed and reliable, in the sense that Chinese companies can expect its objectives to receive fiscal support.

When everything else is changing all the time, the government is a source of stability in a VUCA world. The CCP takes the long view. Because it has no need to renew its mandate every five years or so, it approaches its goals step-by-step, feeling the shape and texture of each stone as it crosses the river.

Entrepreneurs

China has a large public sector, consisting mostly of huge, central, state-owned enterprises (CSOEs), run by civil servants. It is very ineffi- cient by most measures, but this is partly because the CSOEs are obliged to play welfare roles. China's private sector is much smaller than the public sector, but is growing fast. It consists of three types of enterprise: indigenous, first or second generation family-owned small and medium- sized companies; companies set up by entrepreneurs trained in Europe or the US, known as 'sea-turtles', who believe 'west is best' in manage- ment; and firms run by men and women, some of whom are sea-turtles, who believe that although 'west may be best in the West' it is not in China, and are running their firms without management textbooks in ways that seem suited to the Chinese environment.

It is from this latter category that a distinctively Chinese style of management is emerging.

The American economist Israel Kirzner tried to integrate a quality that he called 'entrepreneurial alertness' into classical economic theory. He said that, although it is hard to measure, it should be seen as the fourth factor of production alongside land, labour and capital.

The belief that entrepreneurs embody a scarce economic resource is shared by one of China's most illustrious entrepreneurs, Ma Yun (better known by his westernized name, Jack Ma), who says that the scarcest resource is not money, but entrepreneurial spirit, dreams and values.

Western entrepreneurs and business leaders talk about business and management, but rarely venture opinions on other subjects. Many of China's entrepreneurs talk openly and often about spirituality and morality, and how their management styles reflect, and are aligned with, China's culture.

It's as if they feel a need in China's socialist market economy to estab- lish their credentials as true sons and daughters of China, rather than renegade representatives of an alien American culture and to demon- strate that what they are doing is consistent with, and respects, Chinese culture.

In a 10-page article about Jack Ma in the business magazine, *Green Herald*, a reader who knew nothing about Ma's e-commerce company,

Alibaba, had to wait until page seven for a clue to its business. Before that readers were informed that, not for the first time, Ma had begun an Alibaba presentation in 2009 in Guangzhou, dressed in traditional robes, with a display of his mastery of *tai chi quan* (shadow boxing); that he teaches *tai chi*, *Jinyu* ('keeping silent') and *jingzuo* ('meditation') to his top executives; and believes the hardest tasks for an entrepreneur are to 'rise above the self' and retain a habit of introspection while adapting to an ever-changing world.[2]

China's increasingly self-confident entrepreneurs see, in American management, not a business philosophy, but a useful collection of tools and techniques, some of which need to be adapted to suit the Chinese environment, and an organization (the joint stock company) that gives them access to global capital markets and makes it easy to engage with foreign companies and the global economy.

The American model was just an overlay on China's ancient merchant tradition. It has been a catalyst for China's emergence as a major industrial power, but is now in the process of being retro-fitted into Chinese culture. The result of the retro-fit will be a hybrid – a mixture of western and Chinese. Or, as Jack Ma has suggested, a blend of eastern wisdom, western operational practices and global marketing.

Nine qualities

In his earlier book, the author suggested that the management style emerging in China was being generated by the interplay of 'spirit, land and energy'. 'Spirit' is the cultural substrate underpinning Chinese business philosophy and management – the *I Ching*, Daoism, Confucianism. 'Land' is the environment, including the government. Since the 1978 'great opening', land has become progressively more volatile, uncertain, complex and ambiguous (VUCA). 'Energy' is the entrepreneurial energy that Deng unleashed.

The author argued that the interplay of 'spirit, land, energy' has endowed Chinese management with nine distinctive qualities.

First, it's *dynamic*.

Chinese managers see their environment as in a state of more or less permanent flux. This is partly because of the central role movement plays in the Chinese world-view, and partly because the business environment in China *is* more fluid and turbulent than in the West. China's industries are still at a relatively early stage in their development. There are still lots of opportunities, empty niches and growth potential, particularly in China itself.

In the new VUCA world, the challenge for managers is not to achieve equilibrium adaptation to a stable environment, as Michael Porter urged, but to keep their balance in an environment where there's no prospect of equilibrium.

Chinese managers have visions, but they are fuzzy. The fuzziness of the vision, combined with the turbulence of the environment, usually leads to periods of frenetic activity, interspersed by periods of calm. Chinese managers value action and patience. But it's an aggressive patience: the patience of a sprinter waiting for the starting gun.

Second, it's *adapted*.

Although there is no equilibrium, the business environment has its cycles and seasons. Action is necessary when it's necessary. Fruit will fall when it is ripe.

Government creates some of these rhythms. The five-year plans provide companies with a strategic background, to which their own plans must be aligned. Managers see themselves as parts of their environment. Nothing's created for them. If they are to create value, they must align their rhythms with the environment's.

Third, it's *flexible*.

In a turbulent, unpredictable, VUCA world, you cannot afford to be too wedded to a strategy. Chinese managers can be precise when it is necessary to be precise, but they also value the flexibility of imprecision. If you have no plan, you have no face to lose when it seems necessary to change direction.

Strategy plays only a minor role in Chinese business. It's more of an outcome than an input, a way of rationalising after the event, a series of short-term reactions and adaptations.

Chinese managers tend to juggle with several opportunities at once and may give a visitor the impression there's 'stop' and 'go', but no focus: that where you would expect a strategy, there is a space where balls of opportunity and threat are bobbing about.

The company's next step will depend on which ball falls first, and that will depend on what happens: what events intrude on the fuzzy space of possibilities, and knock a particular ball to the ground. A company's development proceeds, not by the implementation of a strategy, but by a sequence of small steps, each of which opens up new possibilities.

A vision is necessary to steer in roughly the right direction, but the accuracy of the course is less important than the alertness of the look-outs.

Fourth, it's *synthetic.*

The Chinese management style has absorbed and adapted to, and will continue to absorb and adapt to, the principles, tools and techniques of other styles. There's no 'not invented here' syndrome, as there has been in America. Chinese managers share Deng's view – if a cat can catch mice, its colour and provenance are immaterial.

So far the American management style has been the most influential import, but it is easy to exaggerate its impact. The fact that you hear American business school jargon, and frequent references to strategy in business circles, shouldn't be taken as evidence of the depth of American influence on Chinese business thinking.

Fifth, it's *mutual.*

Feng Jun's original nickname in China's personal computer industry was 'five yuan Feng' after he cut the profit margin on his PC key-boards from the standard 50 yuan to 5 yuan. Feng now prefers to be known as 'six wins Feng'.

Feng's idea in 1998, after the market for his 'Little Sun' products had been invaded by a plague of fakes, was to set out the basis of the relationships between his company and what might be called in the west its 'stakeholders.' Henceforth, he announced, his company would be run in a way that reconciled the reasonable interests of six constituencies:

the 'public', by which he meant his customers, distributors, employees, suppliers, the company itself and society at large.

The idea that the company is one of a group of constituencies that depend on one another and have mutual interests in, and claims on, value created, is in tune with the importance in Chinese culture of reciprocal obligations. Feng's inclusion of society in his six interested constituencies also reflects the belief of many Chinese entrepreneurs that they're contributing to the strength of China.

Sixth, it's *consensual.*

If you look at the distribution of power in China through western eyes you see tyranny everywhere, from the all-powerful CCP and its local 'party bosses' to the patriarchs in families and bosses in companies. In terms of the structure of Chinese companies, this perception is accurate enough, but it is misleading because it obscures a key difference in the occidental and Chinese meanings of the word 'boss'.

Three millennia of dynastic rule in China have instilled the shape of hierarchy in the national psyche, presided over by emperors and leaders. The boss plays a key role in the well-ordered Confucian society, but the position has obligations attached. The mandate to rule is conditional on the ruler's good behaviour.

This has two consequences.

- Firstly, leaders recognize the claims of employees on the value they help to create.
- Secondly, although the boss makes the decisions, he or she will only do so after lengthy discussions with advisers and representatives.

Seventh, it's *spiritual.*

It would strike employees of a western company as odd if their CEO invoked a higher spiritual power to explain the company's purpose. Shareholders might also be uneasy if their agent was committed to purposes other than maximising shareholder value.

It is not that westerners are less religious than the Chinese. The evidence indicates the opposite. It is that, in the West, business operates in a material world separate from the spiritual world. As Jack Ma's company presentations illustrate, a company adapted to the Chinese environment is, by definition, a spiritual, as well as a material institution.

Eighth, it's *disciplined.*

Although fuzzy in its logic and spiritual in its communication, the emerging Chinese management style is very far from easy-going. The typical leadership system consists of a CEO and an inner circle of advisers, supported by a well-staffed Chairman's Office, or *dong ban*, which includes a discipline department. Personnel performance reviews are frequent. Staff training is extensive and regimented.

Ninth and last, it's *natural.*

All management styles are 'natural', in the sense that they emerge and are not intentionally designed. But they emerge in particular places and at particular times. The management style that Chinese entrepreneurs adopted during the 30-year American experiment first emerged in mid-19th century America. At that time, in that place, it can be said to have been invoked by its environment.

But early 21st century China is very different from mid-19th century America. If the slate of history could be wiped clean, it's highly unlikely that China today would invoke a management style the same as, or even similar to, the American style. The slate can't be wiped clean – the Chinese management style will be forever marked by its youthful adoption of the American style – but it can be adapted to its environment.

Naturalizing management

The Chinese management style is being naturalized – growing closer to the style that would have emerged if China had eschewed the US economic model. It is becoming 'natural' in another sense, too. It is emerging from the VUCA environment.

It is complicated, because it is a bridge between the rational and the emotional, the tangible and the intangible, the material and the spiritual. It is subtle because it is sensitive to cycles, seasons and the environment. It is fuzzy and difficult to master. To use a word much overused in the West, it's 'organic' and likely to create its own 'ecosystem' in China and perhaps further afield.

The western and Chinese approaches to management both work, in the sense that both have produced successful global companies. But the interesting question is which approach, the strategy-heavy western approach or the strategy-light Chinese approach, is most suited to modern business conditions?

Advocates of the western style will insist that a misty vision, pursued with fuzzy logic, is no substitute for a well-executed strategy and that Chinese companies can't hope to be globally competitive while they remain so strategically delinquent.

Others say that in a VUCA world a strategy is a liability, because it reduces the organization's agility and adaptability.

The problem with strategies is that they are inflexible plans, for unknowable futures. They are attempts to stabilize organizations (and so make them less agile, flexible, alert and creative) in an increasingly turbulent and unpredictable world.

A flawed but instructive experiment

As an experiment in business adaptation to the VUCA world, China's economic miracle is deeply flawed. It is very hard to say which of the nine qualities summarized above (and to what extents), are the consequences of adaptation to the VUCA world, and which are simply the creatures of the interplay between spirit, land and energy.

Some things are clear, however. The origins of China's economy and industries date back to 1978, the dawn of the VUCA age. The energy that has driven China's growth is the same entrepreneurial energy that drives all economic development everywhere. The distinctive philosophical substrate from which Chinese management has emerged is peculiarly suited to the VUCA age. The 1978 adoption by China's otherwise authoritarian government of a policy of extreme economic liberalism has given China's entrepreneurs a relatively free rein in their development of a management style adapted to the business context in modern China.

Some will say that if China is where we're all heading as we adapt to the VUCA world, things can only get worse: enormous and growing inequality, unethical business practices, rampant corruption and alarming levels of air and water pollution. Who needs that? Surely it's better to stick with what we have? But we cannot stick with what we have, and the much discussed 'collateral damage' associated with China's economic miracle is not symptomatic of China. It's the consequence of China's explosive growth since 1978, its adoption of unfettered US-style capitalism as its industrial model and the problems any government would have in establishing more or less from scratch in 1978 the institutions required to regulate an enormous economy.

It seems fair to say that although the Chinese management style is not perfectly adapted to the VUCA world, it is much better adapted to VUCA than the western management style. This is corroborated by the fact that, taken together, the nine distinctive qualities of the Chinese management style summarized above, particularly 'dynamic', 'adapted', 'consensual', and 'flexible', bear more than a passing resemblance to the 'purer' experiment in VUCA adaptation discussed earlier: President Obama's new military doctrine.

---

[1] *China's Management Revolution: Spirit, Land, Energy*: Palgrave Macmillan, 2011.

[2] 'How will Jack Ma Achieve a Greater Alibaba?': *Green Herald*, September 5, 2009.

Chapter 5

Light footprint

In his book, *Confront and Conceal*, published shortly before the US presidential election in November 2012, David Sanger said Obama's use of drones, cyber weapons and special forces amounted to what he called a 'light footprint' strategy designed to protect America's national security interests while avoiding 'protracted ground wars that drained American blood and treasure . . .'.[1]

The light footprint approach seems to have a lot going for it. It is much cheaper than conventional warfare, it puts fewer military personnel at risk, it inflicts less collateral damage and it makes better use of America's technological advantage.

For these and other reasons Obama's 'light footprint' approach is particularly well-adapted to the VUCA world, where fast, focused, clinical interventions, that often take the enemy by surprise, are at a premium.

But it is not without problems and risks.

David Rothkopf, chief executive of *Foreign Policy* magazine and an official in the Clinton administration, is worried about the legal and constitutional aspects of the new policy: 'It is arguable', he says, 'that, through covert wars, this administration has violated the sovereignty of more countries, more times than any other [US] administration'.[2] The covert nature of the stratagems lies at the heart of the problem. By their nature, they are all secret and have to be prosecuted in secret, without oversight or debate.

The ethics of using UCAVs, with their evocation of sentient killer machines in the dystopian vision depicted in the *Terminator* films, have been called into question. It has also been pointed out that they kill good guys too. The New America Foundation, a Washington think-tank, has estimated that 15–16% of the 3,000 or so killed by UCAV attacks since 2004 were non-combatants. This proportion might have been higher if manned aircraft had been used on the same UCAV missions, but for some people, using machines to kill your enemies is ignoble and at odds with the martial tradition.

Kurt Volker, a former US ambassador to NATO, made the point with a rhetorical question: 'What do we want to be as a nation? A country with a permanent kill list? . . . A country that instructs workers in some high-tech operations centre to kill human beings on the far side of the planet, because some government agency determined that those individuals are terrorists?'[3]

Much the same applies to cyber warfare. Martial tradition requires soldiers to put themselves in harm's way. It seems contrary to the unwritten rules of honourable warfare to launch an attack with no prospect of immediate retaliation. And cyber weapons can also harm the innocent, when they spread through the cloud and inadvertently infiltrate and damage non-combatant devices and systems.

Moreover, cyber wars can never be won. New weapons will invoke new counter-measures. It is equivalent to the constant battle between immune systems and pathogens. To engage in cyber warfare is to set a precedent and invite retaliation. It's another arms race run in software labs by the smartest systems designers on the planet.

If the 'fifth domain' of cyberspace is a permanent addition to the thea-tres of war, could the opposite be true of the special forces? Some argue that their time has come and gone; that the period of what Robert Fry called 'strategic broken-play' that followed 9/11, in which the speed, agility and opportunism of special forces were invaluable, is drawing to a close, and a new set of more coherent military challenges associated with nuclear proliferation, and the possibility of wars over resources, is emerging.[4]

Others in the military take a very different view. They see broken play as a permanent feature of the environment and speed, agility and oppor-tunism as essential qualities in all conceivable futures. This is the VUCA vision.

The Bush administration's shift from the 'shock and awe' to 'light foot-print' was motivated largely by economic considerations. President Obama's adoption and rapid development of the LFP approach seems to have been driven not by economic considerations, but by his conviction that this is the way warfare is going and that it is better to be in the forefront than to be playing catch-up.

He may have felt he had no choice. His decisions have affected the speed and sequence of developments, but, in the ultimate analysis, he has been adapting to circumstances and to environmental changes driven by technological advances beyond his control as well as the growing complexity of the modern world. Superpowers cannot shape the world these days, they can only adapt to it.

The problems and risks accompanying the light footprint model are formidable but they must be resolved or accommodated. There is no going back to a simpler world where speaking softly while carrying a big stick solved most international relations problems.

Businesses can learn from this sea change in the military doctrine of the Western Alliance, because many of the environmental changes that have inspired it affect them too. Clearly not all the stratagems of Obama's light footprint approach can be applied to business, but the lightness of foot, the speed and precision, and the use of small, empowered, well-informed teams equipped with state-of-art technology, are characteristics of good management in a VUCA business world.

Light footprint business

Obama realized, and business leaders should realize, that in a VUCA world it's better to stand down the big battalions and to be ready to act quickly whatever happens in a precisely targeted, clinical way that minimizes collateral damage.

The instances of the US military's 'light footprint' (LFP) policy described in Chapter 2 suggest models and modes of operating for modern companies that are more suitable in a VUCA environment than conventional approaches.

Unmanned

There was always going to come a time when the 'off-shoring' trend that has been such a prominent feature of globalization would be reversed by what economists call factor-substitution (substituting capital, in the form of automation, for labour). If the motivation to 'off-shore' manufacturing was a desire to take advantage of the labour costs in Low Cost Countries (LCCs), advances in industrial robotics were bound to reach a point where labour costs were such a small proportion of total costs that the economics of off-shoring became marginal and eventually negative.

The current trend towards 're-shoring' or 'home-sourcing' is being driven by rising LCC labour costs, high oil prices, smaller lot sizes because of uncertainty, shorter product life-cycles and customization. It is hard to say whether automation is driving or enabling the trend towards the repatriation. Either way, suppliers of robots are enjoying it.

Figures from the International Federation of Robotics show 165,000 robots were sold in 2011, an increase of over a third on 2010 and the highest figure ever recorded. In what amounts to an automation 'arms race', the number of robots in China increased by 42% in 2011. Foxconn, which makes iPhones and iPads in huge factories in Taiwan and China, plans to replace a million workers with robots. According to the Chinese site, Techweb, each so-called 'Foxbot' costs $20–25,000, over three times the average salary of Foxconn's mostly Chinese employees, whose wages have been rising sharply in recent years.

So-called '3-D printing', combined with Computer Aided Design, and Manufacturing (CAD/CAM) software, Computer Numerically Controlled (CNC) machine tools and Web-based manufacturing networks have all ushered in an era of remote-controlled design, testing, and product development and 'distributed manufacturing' that allows companies to produce close to their customers. This reduces logistics costs and permits closer adaptation to local markets and growing demands for customization.

It is not just process engineering. Like drones, many products are also on a steep developmental path towards increased automation and autonomy. Driverless (remote-controlled and autonomous) cars are a decade or so away, and consumer durables are getting smarter every year.

LFP companies are gluttons for robotics and automation, because these processes give them flexibility, reduce their industrial relations as well as their logistics costs, free up employees for higher value uses and help prepare them for what may be a totally different future to the one they had envisaged.

But using the latest in robotics, automation and digitalization is not an end in itself. It is part of a journey towards ever lighter and more agile organizations.

Like the military's remote-controlled drones, robots and automation systems are getting smarter, but, as with drones, it is a 'bottom-up' process; a steady accumulation of sensitivities and abilities in response to users' needs and constant technological advance. Simularly, it seems possible that this bottom-up development of robots and automation will lead to what has come to be known as the 'technological singularity': the emergence of true artificial intelligences (AIs).

Because it is hard to predict, or even to imagine, what AIs will be capable of, their emergence, some time this century, is being seen as an 'event horizon' beyond which subsequent developments cannot be predicted. It seems likely, however, that organizations with an appetite for automation and unmanned facilities and products today will be well placed to survive and thrive beyond tomorrow's event horizon (see box below).

Existential threats

Ray Kurzweil, a distinguished American futurologist, predicts that at some point in the next 30 years we will build our last machine. This machine will be so smart that it and its successors will build all subsequent machines, and each will be smarter than the last.

Kurzweil calls the point the 'singularity' and believes it will be a change 'comparable to the rise of human life on Earth'.[5] In collaboration with Google and NASA's Ames Research Center, Kurzweil opened the Singularity University in 2009 to 'educate and inspire a cadre of leaders ... to understand and facilitate the development of exponentially advancing technologies and apply, focus and guide these tools to address humanity's grand challenges'.

Kurzweil is a former director of the Singularity Institute founded by Eliezer Yudkowsky in 2000, with backing from PayPal co-founder, Peter Thiel. Its aim is to ensure that the singularity, when it occurs, takes the form of a 'friendly AI' (artificial intelligence) rather than a competitor with humans.

A less sanguine view of the singularity has inspired the formation of the Centre for the Study of Existential Risk in Cambridge in the UK by Jaan Tallinn, co-founder of Skype, Huw Price, professor of philosophy at Cambridge University, and Lord Rees, Astronomer Royal, master of Trinity College, Cambridge, a former president of the Royal Society and author of *Our Final Century?: Will the Human Race Survive the Twenty-first Century?*.[6]

The centre will study all 'existential' risks (risks that threaten human life on Earth), including pandemics and catastrophic climate change as well as the AI singularity.

Jack Welch, the former boss of General Electric and among the best-known industrialists of his time, said in the 1980s that companies must decide whether to 'automate, emigrate, or evaporate'. Because automation reduces the benefits of emigration, the choice today is starker: 'automate or evaporate.'[7]

The Fifth Domain

In the spring of 2008 Dave Carroll and his band mates from *Sons of Maxwell* were flying to Nebraska for a one-week tour. Before take-off, Carroll saw United Airlines (UA) baggage handlers damage his $3,500 guitar, by throwing it into the hold of the airplane. After a year of fruit-less conversations with UA customer-service staff, Carroll turned to the Web. The first of three songs he wrote about his experience – featuring the lyrics 'United, some big help you are. You broke it, you should fix it. You're liable, just admit it. I should have flown with someone else or gone by car, because United breaks guitars' – and accompanied by a video on YouTube, spread like wildfire through Facebook and attracted nearly half a million hits in two days (*Montreal Gazette*, July 10, 2009).

The following day, the airline announced that it was entering into 'conversations' with Carroll to 'make things right' and said later that the incident was 'a unique learning opportunity that we would like to use for training purposes, to ensure all customers receive better service from us'.

The tale of Carroll's guitar illustrates, according to some public relations specialists, how social media has ushered in a new age of consumer power in which anyone with a grudge or a complaint can name and shame corporations online. Websites devoted to the sins of omission and commission of particular companies have been around for years, of course, but social media gives Web criticisms a sharper edge, because it spreads them much more quickly and much more widely.

It is the flip-side of so-called 'viral marketing', commonly used by companies to promote their products cheaply to much smaller market segments than was previously possible. Social media is a powerful new tool for corporate marketers: but it is an equally powerful weapon for corporate critics.

With such 'reputational' risks lurking in social media, waiting to ambush the unwary, some companies decide discretion is the better part of valour and steer well clear. But that's not a real option. You have to listen and watch 24/7 in any event for leaks, accusations and other attacks or criticisms, warranted or unwarranted. And the best way to counter an attack that could go viral is to engage in the conversation and publish an anti-virus. Social media is much more than a new source of marketing opportunities. It is a new, permanent space where reputational assets and liabilities are being created and destroyed more or less constantly.

Although social media mostly consists of the trivial, banal and mundane, it can contain valuable information for marketers with the patience and tools needed to extract it. In September 2011, Derwent Capital Markets in London launched a £25m fund that invests according to whether people are happy, sad, anxious or tired. The system uses an algorithm designed by Johan Bollen, professor of informatics and computing at Indiana University in the US (*Sunday Times*, September 11, 2011).

The algorithm takes a randomly sampled 10% of all tweets, compares positive with negative comments and then uses a program designed by

Google to define six moods: calm, alert, sure, vital, kind and happy. In a study published in October 2010, Bollen used a Twitter feed to predict with an accuracy of 88% the direction of the daily price movements of Dow Jones index constituents. Bollen's initial hypothesis was that mood swings would follow Dow Jones index price movements, but he found it was the other way round: a worsening of mood in the online community preceded a fall in stock prices.

According to von Clausewitz war is, 'nothing more than the continuation of politics by other means'. Use of cyber weapons, such as Stuxnet (see Chapter 2), is illegal in business, of course, but just as industrial espionage and sabotage (the continuation of competition by other means) are not unknown in the physical business world, the possibility of their use in the virtual world cannot be ruled out entirely. Appropriate defences must be erected and appropriate dispositions made.

A 2012 UK 'Information Security Breaches Survey' by PwC found that 93% of large companies and 76% of small businesses had suffered a cyber security breach in the previous year. Jonathan Evans, director-general of MI5, the UK military intelligence organization, said an un-named large, listed UK company had come under a state-sponsored cyber attack that had cost it £800m in lost revenue.[7] In late 2012, Saudi Aramco, the world's largest oil producer, revealed that a virus called Shamoon had affected 30,000 desktop computers in an attack on the company's oil production operations. Shamoon is also reported to have attacked Qatar's RasGas group, one of the world's largest producers of Liquefied Natural Gas.[8]

Cyberspace is the 'fifth domain' of warfare. It is also one of the domains of business competition, alongside finance and innovation. It is not simply a new way to market. It is a new, vast, extremely complex, largely independent, rapidly evolving competitive domain, with its own heroes and villains.

Special forces

In the conventional organization, armies of specialists, working in accordance with minutely specified processes, execute the tasks demanded of them. The soldiers of the armies may never meet, and will often live and work on opposite sides of the world. No one but the leadership sees the whole work, and it's not even necessary for contributors to the work to know its aim or ultimate purpose.

In highly automated LFP companies, fewer, less specialized people do higher value-added work. Each is trained in a number of skills and works in a small, autonomous team. The team is the unit of agency. The team members together possess most, if not all, of the skills required to execute whatever tasks are assigned to the team. Teams are psychologically integrated with their own *esprits de corps* and collectively motivated. They are self-adjusting, self-directed and self-improving.

The interconnections between the teams and external individuals or organizations make this arrangement complex. But complexity within the organization is a virtue in a VUCA world because its makes an organization more agile and adaptable. And, in any case, the greater complexity of the organizational form is offset by the autonomy of the teams, which require less central management.

Unlike the departments and functions of conventional companies, the constituent teams of LFP companies are not the slaves of processes dispensed from high. They do their own thing in their own way and are motivated to find new ways of doing things that produce better results, with fewer resources.

Although not directed much from the outside, each team is aware of its internal and external customers and suppliers and takes pains to establish and maintain mutually advantageous relationships with each of them, and with the organization as a whole.

Companies organized in this modular way tend to react more quickly to opportunities and threats, to squander fewer resources and to be more adaptable and innovative than conventional companies. They also tend to be better attuned to the needs and desires of clients and customers, and better at collaborating with other companies or individuals.

The LFP company's organizational power, or 'Gemba Power' as it is known in Japan (see Chapter 7), is the sum of the Gemba Power of its teams. The leaders of LFP organizations play a role not unlike that of the managers of a holding company and apply the principle of 'subsidiarity': don't do anything that can be done just as well, if not better, by the team.

LFP organizations replace 'big battalions' as their prime units of agency with small, well-trained, well-equipped, agile and flexible self-managing teams or groups. In a sense their structure is their strategy, although LFP companies do not set much store by strategy as the word is usually understood.

Operation Hit Back

A global dairy products group with strong brands was doing well in a Latin American country. Gross revenue was growing at 20% a year and the group's leading brands were becoming firmly established in the marketplace.

But the growth was uneven and had petered out completely in a few big cities. The generally accepted view was that this was only to be expected. Competition tended to be more intense in big cities because competitors targeted them first. The company's brands were simply finding their natural level. There was nothing to be done.

Sheila Regan (not her real name), Vice President of yoghurt business lines in Latin America, was not inclined to accept that state of affairs. But she chose not to throw tons of money into media marketing to prove her point. Instead, she gathered as much information as she could with quantitative and qualitative research and anecdotal evidence.

Armed with this in-depth knowledge of the 'big city' problem, Regan mounted a precisely targeted intervention in one of the big cities where growth was faltering. It came to be known as 'Operation Hit Back'. 'We didn't want to push all the levers,' she recalled, 'just those related to 48 target stores we had identified. We focused on the right channels, the 48 stores, and the key brands. We stopped buying media, and invested instead in in-store promotions. The 48 target stores received special treatment, to help our sales people to deliver perfect service. To avoid stock-outs, for example, they were always served first. This wasn't just marketing and sales. It was a business approach.'

It was also a surreptitious approach. The target stores were never told they were getting special treatment. Regan was anxious not to alert competitors to what they were up to because they could have taken countermeasures. One of the main objectives of the operation was to persuade new entrants that the incumbents were too strong to make the investments they would need to gain a foothold in the market worthwhile.

A dedicated, cross-functional team was assembled including supply and logistics specialists and someone from finance to make sure the operation was profitable. A dedicated Operation Hit Back 'war room' was established in the country's head office.

The room had a 'war wall' showing the 48 target stores, along with their objectives and the impact of the interventions. When a store went from red to green, indicating its objectives had been met, cheers broke out in the war room. 'It had a snow-ball effect,' said Regan. 'By sharing results we encouraged the others, and could apply best practices quickly.'

The intimacy of the war room, and the visible engagement of senior leaders, promoted a trusting, learning atmosphere in which instant sharing of best practices and continuous improvement (*kaizen*, as the Japanese call it) became the norm. 'I was the godmother,' said Regan. 'I was there when we selected stores, when we decided where to focus our efforts, and when we set up the war wall. When senior executives visited us, we put them to work on the project.

'The teams saw us regularly. To show them they had our support and commitment, we visited the target stores, giving encouragement and feedback.'

The results were remarkable. Before Operation Hit Back began, gross revenues in the target city were falling at a rate of 1.5% a year. By the time Regan left the city and returned to Europe, carrying a framed picture of herself and the Operation Hit Back team signed by all the members, gross revenues in the target city were growing at 17.8% a year.

Regan's intervention model and its results were studied with great interest at the global head office and, at the time of writing, it seems likely that the approach, with its use of in-depth analysis and precisely targeted interventions by a dedicated, multi-skilled team would be 'rolled out' to other major cities.

Post-strategic Apple

The LFP approach isn't a 'strategy' in the normal sense. It's more a philosophy, an approach, a style or a mode of operating than a strategy. If you cannot predict what is going to happen and if you know that whatever you and others do is bound to have unintended consequences, there is no point in drawing up a detailed long-term plan.

The LFP approach is to react quickly – to seize and respond to all opportunities and threats as decisively and clinically as possible, with the minimum of collateral damage. Tactical responses within a guiding vision of some kind, rather than grand strategies, are the two features that distinguish LFP management most clearly from the conventional management wisdom.

Some of the elements of the LFP management approach are evident in the new management style emerging in China's private sector (see Chapter 4). One could say the Chinese government governs in an LFP way because it knows from bitter experience that, in a nation of 1.3 billion people, the consequences of major mistakes such as the Great Leap Forward can be horrendous.

The dominance of strategy in the contemporary management discourse obscures the role played by other approaches. Because strategy is everything, every success is interpreted as strategic. It's in the interests of none of the key actors (CEOs, strategy consultants or business schools) to attribute business success to anything other than good strategy, and particularly not to something as prosaic as luck or opportunism.

We are fortunate, therefore, that a book on how one of the world's most successful companies has been managed over the past 25 years has been written by someone who is not a management writer. Walter Isaacson, who had previously written much-admired lives of Albert Einstein and Benjamin Franklin, published his biography of Apple's CEO, the late Steve Jobs, in 2011.[9]

When embarking on the two-year project, Isaacson was unburdened by any preconceptions about how businesses are, or ought to be, run. He told the Jobs tale as he saw it, as it was told to him in over 40 interviews with the man himself, and over 100 conversations with those who knew him, including family members, friends, colleagues and competitors.

Isaacson wasn't particularly interested in business. *Steve Jobs* is about a man, not a management style. And yet, from a book untainted by a word of management 'speak', a management narrative emerges. It's one quite unlike the supposedly standard strategy-led management.

Pixar

When Jobs bought 70% of Lucasfilm's computer division in 1986 shortly after his resignation from Apple, the main attraction was the Pixar Image Computer, from which the new stand-alone company, part-owned by its employees, took its name. It sold for $125,000, to graphic designers and animators mainly, but also to the medical industry for 3-D CAT scanning and to the military for rendering images from satellites and reconnaissance flights.

The business had two other less tangible attractions for Jobs. The first was that Pixar's hardware was designed around its software – particularly its Reyes rendering program – and Jobs recognized the virtue of a high degree of hardware/software integration. Second, it straddled the borders between technology and art; an interface where most technologists and most artists feel uncomfortable, but where Jobs was in his element.

He initially tried to persuade his colleagues to widen the markets for the Pixar hardware and software by producing cheaper, cut-down versions of the image computer and Reyes. He believed people would find 'clever new ways to use tools ... the inventor never imagined'. Cyber-punk author William Gibson had the same thought: 'the street finds its own uses for technology.'

Jobs didn't press the point and Pixar's hardware and software were not adapted for the mass market. They did, however, lead to a B2B (business to business) relationship that would bear fruit later in an unexpected area. When Roy Disney, Walt's nephew, wanted to reboot Disney's animation division, he asked Pixar to help. Pixar developed a suite of animation tools for Disney, first used in 1988 in *The Little Mermaid*.

Pixar's digital animation division was originally designed to show off its systems, but, as luck would have it, it was led by the very talented John Lasseter, with whom Jobs forged a strong bond. Jobs was delighted when, *Luxor*, Lasseter's short animated film about a parent and child table lamp won the 'best film' award at an annual computer graphics conference in 1986.

While the main business struggled, Jobs protected Lasseter and his team from cost cuts and agreed to finance another short film, *Tin Toy*. In 1988 it became the first computer-generated film to win an Academy Award for short animated films.

Disney liked *Tin Toy* and tried to entice Lasseter away from Pixar to lead its animation division. But Lasseter was loyal to Jobs and Pixar. Disney's CEO, Michael Eisner, settled for an agreement with Jobs for Pixar to make a film for Disney. The rest is history: *Toy Story*, *A Bug's Life*, *Toy Story 2*, *Monsters Inc.*, *Finding Nemo*, *The Incredibles* and, after Disney's $7.4bn acquisition of Pixar in 2005, *Cars*, *Ratatouille*, *WALL-E*, *Up*, *Toy Story 3* and *Cars 2*.

Not much 'strategy' here. Rather the acquisition of an animation hardware and software company by a man with a liking for the technology/ art interface. A friendship between the acquirer and an artist working on the marketing side. Awards for the latter's animated films at a time when the pioneer of animated films was struggling. All of which seems more like a random walk by an inspired opportunist unburdened by a plan or strategy.

Apple

Following Jobs's return to Apple in 1997 after Apple's purchase of his computer company, NeXT, his first task was a 'no brainer': to inject some of the old Apple magic back into the product line. That task was completed the following year with the launch and sales success of the iMac personal computer, designed by Jonathan Ive under the watchful eye of the Jobs 'Techo-Zen' aesthetic.

What to do next?

The conventional answer was to hire top-level consultants, analyze the PC market and develop a strategy for increasing Apple's market share.

Targets and milestones would be set, supply chains re-configured and change programmes devised and implemented.

That wasn't Jobs's way.

In the aftermath of the bursting of the dot.com bubble in 2000 the 'top 100 people' at Apple decided, at their annual think-in, that the hitherto self-sufficient PC was morphing into something else – into what they dubbed a 'digital hub', co-ordinating other devices such as cameras, video recorders and music players.

The key enabling technology was FireWire, a high-speed serial port Apple had developed in the early 1990s, which moved files from one device to another. When Adobe declined Jobs's request to write its Premiere and PhotoShop software for the iMac, Apple developed its own versions. If Adobe had complied with the request, history might have been different, because Apple wouldn't have achieved the same level of hardware/software integration in its non-PC product line.

The digital hub model was first applied to video. Video files were transferred, via FireWire, to the Mac, where iMovie was waiting to discharge its editing duties. Next came a drive that could burn a DVD, with iDVD. Photos followed, with iPhoto and then, belatedly, Apple's attention turned to music. In 2000, 320 million blank CDs were sold in the US in a sudden explosion of music 'ripping' from CDs and downloading from file-sharing sites such as Napster. Apple wasn't in the game.

The catch-up campaign began with a CD burner on the iMac, but that was not enough. Jobs wanted to make it easy to transfer music from a CD, manage it on the iMac and burn playlists. Other firms were already supplying such music-management systems, but Jobs judged them to be clumsy and excessively complicated. Apple got into the game by buying SoundJam, a small start-up company founded by three Apple alumni.

The Apple-ized SoundJam was launched as iTunes in January, 2001 as part of the digital hub idea. It was free to all Mac users. If the then current generation of digital music players had been better, more advanced with more storage, that might have been as close as Apple got to the hardware world beyond the computer. But MP3 music players in 2001 were primitive, complicated and far from capacious.

Jobs and his colleagues knew what 'good' would look like in an MP3 player, but the wish was not father to the reality. The components were not readily available. They found a suitable LCD screen and a re-chargeable lithium battery after a few months, but mass storage small enough for a pocket music player yet sufficient for a 1,000-song playlist, was tomorrow's technology.

Or so project leader Jon Rubinstein thought.

At the end of a routine meeting with Apple's supplier, Toshiba, an engineer mentioned a new product Toshiba was working on, for which a use had yet to be found: a tiny 1.8 inch Winchester drive with a capacity of five gigabytes – enough for 1,000 songs. Rubinstein was hard put to keep a poker face. Apple negotiated an exclusive deal to buy all the drives Toshiba produced. The iPod was launched in September 2001.

The success of the iPod and its derivatives had management experts swooning in the aisles. Brilliant strategy, superbly executed: an exemplification of the transformational power of an inspired plan and peerless 'strategic' leadership. Business schools and strategy consultants were all over it like a rash. Apple's transition from a non-conformist computer manufacturer nibbling round the edges of a market dominated by Windows-based machines into the creator of elegant icons of a new age, was unequivocal corroboration of their world view.

Or was it?

A successful outcome does not necessarily imply the execution of a great strategy. Looking back at the sequence of events that led to Apple's golden iPod-iPad decade reveals very little that could be construed as conventional strategizing.

There was a vision – the personal computer would become a 'digital hub'. It turned out to be pregnant with implications, but all that it implied initially was that Apple should equip its products with CD burner drives and software for managing video, photo and music files. It is true the digital hub made it possible to put 'smarts' on the computer and so enable its supplying devices (camcorders, cameras and music players) to be simpler. But this did not, on its own, oblige Apple to make those supplying devices. It did not make camcorders or cameras. It wanted to make a music player because Jobs and many of his colleagues were keen on music (Jobs was a Bob Dylan fan) and they didn't think much of the digital music players already on the market.

But suppose Rubinstein hadn't heard about Toshiba's tiny drive or suppose Sony had heard of it first and agreed an exclusive supply contract? Suppose the current generation of music players had been better? Suppose Adobe had agreed to write Mac OSX versions of its Premiere and Photoshop software? The 'digital hub' wasn't an Apple invention. By the time Apple gave it a name in 2001 it was a well-established trend that was emerging spontaneously from the broader 'digitalization' of other devices, such as cameras, camcorders and music players.

Strategy? Hardly. Luck, fortunate timing, prepared minds. Adjacent possibilities (iPhone, iPad) opened up by the knowhow acquired and the intellectual property (design themes, brand, etc.) accumulated when taking the previous step. Apple's success wasn't intended. It emerged.

Creative constraints

It wasn't all luck. Apple's golden decade was also the creature of Steve Jobs's visions, beliefs, obsessions, frustrations and taste: his belief in the 'digital hub' future for personal computers; his liking for hardware/software integration and end-to-end control of the customer experience; his rigorous, sometimes brutal insistence on elegant design and operating simplicity; his obsession with the design and technical details; his ability to attract, inspire and retain talented people; and, perhaps above all, the extraordinarily fertile way in which Jobs combined the mind of a technologist with the soul of an artist.

These qualities and attributes screened and filtered the rivers of ideas and possibilities flowing through Apple in the first decade of the 21st century, helped to decide which were chosen to become Apple products and shaped and guided their development processes.

The role of 'leadership' in business success and failure is almost always over-estimated, just as the role of good fortune is almost always underestimated. But Isaacson's book leaves the reader in no doubt that the influence this man had on this enormous company (at the time of writing Apple is the most valuable company in the world) was not inconsiderable. The lean, ascetic Jobs personified Apple: the classy elegance of its stores and packaging, the spare beauty of its products, the sublime simplicity of their engagement with their users.

But he was not a strategic leader; not a planner. He wasn't one to instruct or prescribe. Although the effect of his contribution was usually positive, the currency of his contributions was negatives: 'that sucks', 'this stinks', 'too complicated'. It was the ideas and designs Jobs rejected that made Apple's products distinctive. He was what Edgar Schein called an 'artist leader', a chef tasting the dishes of his associates and judging them be too salty, or too sweet, until one is proffered that's just right.

He was the patriarch: the keeper of the Apple faith and the Apple design philosophy. He didn't tell Apple people what to do but the regard they held him in – and his vantage point above the day-to-day work – gave him the power to proscribe, to tell them when they were barking up the wrong tree, re-inventing the wheel, or heading down roads others had proved to be dead-ends.

Jobs was not the easiest boss the work for. He didn't suffer fools gladly and he was seldom inclined to be diplomatic about his likes and dislikes. But that was OK. Apple people loved him anyway. Jobs was their icon, their ambassador to the outside world. And by and large, they were content with how he represented them (see Chapter 9).

The constraints Jobs imposed liberated and channelled the creative energy of the organization and maintained consistency.

Sixty years before Little, Brown published *Steve Jobs* in the UK, it published another American book Jobs might have read in his youth: J. D. Salinger's classic novel *Catcher in the Rye*. The protagonist and narrator, Holden Caulfield, imagined his role in adult life as guarding children playing in a rye field on the edge of a cliff.

This was not unlike Jobs's role at Apple. For the children playing in the rye field, read creativity, invention and experimentation. For the cliff, read commercial failure. For Holden Caulfield, read Jobs.

Jobs the adaptable

When he bought control of Pixar in 1986, Steve Jobs had no thought of becoming a film-maker. When he returned to Apple in 1997 he had no thought of making anything other than computers, let alone of launching a frontal assault on the mobile phone market. Had he had such aspirations he might not have dismissed them as inappropriate or unrealistic, as others would have in his position. He was a man of enormous self-confidence. He felt no need for strategy consultants or their matrices and would have judged their stricture that firms should 'stick to their knitting' as 'stupid'.

But he had no plan.

He was a Daoist content to 'go with the flow', to adapt to changes in the environment; to his discovery of John Lasseter's genius; to Disney's wish to revive its animation division; to the digital hub idea; to Adobe's refusal to write its software for the Mac OSX; to the indifferent quality of the first generation of MP3 players; to the migration of the music player to the phone; to the opportunity created by the success of the iPod and the iPhone to make a proper, full-function Apple version of the old, half-forgotten idea of the tablet computer.

Going with the flow

In a VUCA business world, each step opens up adjacent possibilities that were non-existent or invisible before the step was taken.

Armed with their assets in the form of people, approaches, know-how and brands, and their relationships with customers, distributors, suppliers and collaborators; guided by misty visions; alert and on the look out for opportunities and threats, ready to act at short notice, LFP companies take random walks into the future. Sometimes their random walks look, in retrospect, like inspired, brilliantly executed strategies, but that is to confuse outcome with intent.

In a VUCA environment, LFP companies often out-perform strategy-led companies because, unconstrained by intentions, they are more open to serendipitous opportunities, are less likely to be wrong-footed by the unexpected and have no reputations to lose if they suddenly change direction.

Before VUCA, tactics supported strategy. In the LFP, VUCA-adapted organization, strategy emerges from tactics.

[1] *Confront and Conceal: Obama's Secret Wars and Surprising Use of American Power:* Crown, 2012.

[2] 'Undeclared and Undiscussed': *Financial Times,* October 22 2012.

[3] 'America's Covert Drone War is Out of Control': *Financial Times,* December 11, 2012.

[4] 'Survival of the Fittest': *Prospect,* November 2012.

[5] 'I robot, you soon to be extinct': *Sunday Times,* November 25, 2012.

[6] William Heinemann, 2003.

[7] 'Cut cyber threat by declaring attacks, companies told': *Financial Times,* December 4, 2012.

[8] 'Saudi cyber attack targeted oil output': *Financial Times,* December 11, 2012.

[9] *Steve Jobs:* Little, Brown, 2011.

Chapter 6

Four characteristics

In addition to its three characteristic stratagems – drones, cyber weapons and special forces – the LFP company's adaptations to VUCA produce two characteristic operating modes and two distinctive qualities.

The characteristic modes are that it operates in a centralized and a decentralized way simultaneously, and prefers partnerships to acquisitions. The distinctive qualities are that it is obliged, by its characteristic stratagems, to be secretive and to accept that its actions, although light, will inevitably cause collateral damage.

Centralized and decentralized

One of the most striking images US President Barack Obama's first administration was of Obama watching television in the White House situation room in May 2011. Obama looks anxious and so do his companions: Vice President Joe Biden, Defence Secretary Robert Gates, Secretary of State Hillary Clinton, Chairman of the Joint Chiefs Admiral Mike Mullen, National Security Adviser Tom Donilon and Counter-Terrorism chief John Brennan. They're watching a real-life thriller in real time via a video camera attached to the helmet of a US Navy SEAL.

No-one talks. There's nothing to say. It was all said a while back, when the President gave the mission the go ahead. They watch as Osama bin Laden is shot in the left eye and then again (the so-called 'double tap') in the chest. Exultation. Vindication (of the LFP idea), justice at last for the architect of the 9/11 attacks, redemption for US special forces three decades after the Operation Eagle Claw humiliation and a decade after bin Laden's escape from Tora Bora.

Obama didn't pull the trigger, didn't approve the killshot, didn't lead the assault on the Abbottabad compound, didn't organize or plan the mission, didn't select the men or their equipment and didn't make any of the thousands of decisions that led up to the moment when someone asked him: 'We've found him. We have a plan. A team's on stand-by. We can get him. Yes, or No?'

Obama in his situation room surrounded by his senior staff, or his *dong ban* as the Chinese call the chairman's staff, exemplifies the characteristic distribution of power in an LFP organization.

The big decisions are made centrally. Every other decision is made locally, on the ground, by the team or teams directly involved; a paradoxical world of extreme decentralization and empowerment and extreme centralization.

But in his role of commander-in-chief of the armed forces Obama is no dictator. He consults with, and heeds the advice of, his staff. He's the tie-breaker, the ultimate agent, the place where the buck no-one else can take has to stop. And he takes responsibility for the consequences of the actions triggered by his decisions. He did not squeeze the trigger in Abbottabad but everyone knows that, without his say so, the trigger would not have been squeezed.

It was the same with Steve Jobs. He did not design the iPod – that was mostly the work of the Englishman, Jonathan ('Jony') Ive – but people see the iPod as Jobs's brain-child because they know that it was his 'techno-Zen' aesthetic that filtered out the rival designs and said 'we'll go with that one' (see Chapter 5).

The conventional wisdom about 'leadership' is that it is an honour awarded by the led, rather than a position conferred by the board: that it's a quality, rather than a title. That is not how it works in an LFP organization. In the LFP organization, there is a formal component in the role of leader. The modules are for the most part self-managing but everyone accepts there is a small proportion of decisions that cannot be made at module level and someone, it does not really matter who, has to take them.

Remember the difference noted in Chapter 4 between the Chinese and occidental meanings of the word 'boss'. The Chinese are accustomed to hierarchies, with emperors or CCP chairmen at the top. But they do not submit to that power unconditionally. The leader's position has obligations attached. The mandate to rule ('Mandate of Heaven', in imperial

China) is conditional on the ruler's good behaviour. A ruler who behaves 'badly', however that is defined, can be opposed and, if necessary, deposed (witness the Jobs-engineered dismissal of John Scully as Apple's CEO).

Chinese CEOs are acutely aware of the conditions attached to their positions and act accordingly. They take pains to ensure everyone has a stake in the success of the business and they never decide on a whim. It is only after long discussions with experts and counsellors that bosses take the decisions that are their responsibility alone.

This polarization of power in LFP organizations leaves little room for full-time managers. Each module manages itself and each member of the module can play a management role if the need arises. With the help of modern technology, the 'boss' and his or her staff can do all the monitoring work. When a CEO has access in real-time to sales discussions, for example and can see the impact of store promotions directly, there is no need for a full-time intermediate management layer.

The success of the Orpheus Chamber Orchestra exemplifies the power and effectiveness of the self-managing module.

Modular music

The orchestra has been seen (by Peter Drucker, doyen of management writers, among others) as a model for business organizations, and conductors, the celebrities of classical music, as role models for CEOs.

In his book *Leadership Ensemble,* Harvey Seifter, the then executive director of the New York-based Orpheus Chamber Orchestra, explains how this unusual institution became a world leading orchestra with no conductor. The Orpheus Orchestra uses a democratic system known as the 'Orpheus process', which takes all the decisions that are made by the conductor in a conventional orchestra.[1]

The process is not easy or efficient in terms of time, but it is very effective. The Orpheus has won several Grammy awards and the quality of its performances allows it to charge higher concert fees than any other chamber orchestra.

When first rehearsing a piece of music, a 'core team' consisting of the principal player for that piece from each instrument section, decides musical elements such as tempo, interpretation, phrasing and bowing. The core team members are the 'leaders', chosen by the orchestra, for that particular piece. 'No one owns a chair; no one owns a principal title,' said executive director Graham Parker. A few hours after the core team has met the full orchestra assembles to rehearse.[2]

In 'the executive', board and orchestra members may have different roles – musicians have administrative roles, staff members sit on orchestra committees. 'We try to mix it up as much as we can,' said Parker.

In his foreword to Seifter's book, Richard Hackman, a professor of social and organizational psychology at Harvard University, asked: 'Rather than relying on a charismatic, visionary leader . . . might it be possible for all members to share responsibility for leadership and for differences and disagreements to be sources of creativity rather than something that should be suppressed in the interest of uniformity and social harmony?'

It has always been that way in 'popular' music: no conductors and rotating leadership from piece to piece. The jazz jamming session exemplifies the self-managing qualities of small groups: not even a score, just a misty musical vision, mutual respect and a shared wish to create something beautiful and original. There are signs, in the more formal, regimented world of classical music, that the self-conducting model is currently mounting a serious challenge to the conventional, conductor-led model. The Orpheus is not alone in dispensing with a conductor (see box below).

Conductor-less orchestras

Perviy Simfonicheskiy Ansambl' bez Dirizhyora (First Conductorless Symphony Ensemble), or *Persimfans*, was formed in Russia in 1922 for political and philosophical motives as much as for musical reasons. It was run by a committee. Musicians sat in a circle while they performed and took their cues across the circle. *Persimfans* was disbanded in 1932, also for political reasons.

The *Prague Chamber Orchestra* was formed in 1951 as a chamber music offshoot of the Czechoslovak Radio Symphony Orchestra (CRSO). The oldest surviving conductor-less orchestra, it became independent of the CRSO in 1965.

The *Orpheus Chamber Orchestra* was formed in 1972 by cellist Julian Fifer. In 1975, another cellist, John Painter, founded the *Australian Chamber Orchestra*. It calls itself an 'ensemble of soloists'. Concertmaster Richard Tognetti was appointed artistic director and lead violin in 1990.

The conductor-less *Amsterdam Sinfonietta* was formed in 1988 and the San Francisco-based 20-member all-string *New Century Chamber Orchestra* conducter-free – was founded in 1992.

In what has all the appearances of a glitch (see Chapter 1) in the classical music firmament, the rate at which conductor-less chamber orchestras are forming has accelerated in recent years. In the US, the conductor-less *East Coast Chamber Orchestra* was formed in 2001, the *Advent Chamber Orchestra* began performing in 2003 and *A Far Cry*, an 18-member string orchestra in Boston, which describes itself as 'self-conducted', and has a rotating leadership system, was formed in 2007. The *Lyra Vivace Chamber Orchestra* of Augusta was founded in 2010, the 29-member *Ars Nova Chamber Orchestra* of Washington DC, a 'self-conducted' orchestra, with rotating leadership where the musicians make the artistic decisions, and help out with marketing and administration, was formed in late 2010 and the conductor-less *Arizona Chamber Orchestra* began performing in 2011.

The conventional wisdom is that an organization can be centralized *or* decentralized, but not both. Yet LFP organizations are centralized and decentralized. It can be confusing and, as some conductor-less orchestras have found, awkward to operate until people get used to it. This is where leaders come in. They are orchestrators, rather than conductors. By personifying and representing the organization, they unleash its decentralized organizational power (see Chapter 9 for more on LFP leadership).

Collaborative

Military alliances are as old as warfare itself but making common cause with those with complementary interests to deter or oppose a shared foe has become a particularly prominent feature of modern military doctrine and practice.

Alliances, mutual defence pacts, coalitions and the use of proxies or principal/agent relationships are a vitally important component of the 'light footprint' approach favoured by President Obama.

At the of time writing, the US is engaged in a full-scale proxy war supporting a multinational African army against Islamist militants in Somalia and is training locals to carry out military missions all over the world. Military personnel take part in numerous joint exercises to nurture alliances and coalitions and train surrogate forces to support US security objectives.

A footprint shared, is a footprint halved, in Obama's view.

The policy maximizes the effectiveness of the military by allowing a small deployment of American troops, often including special forces, to achieve substantial military objectives.

Problems arise with this approach, many of which are to do with the trustworthiness or otherwise of your allies (witness the so-called 'green-on-blue' attacks by allies on US soldiers in Afghanistan). But the risk of defection has always accompanied an alliance and there are no signs that the green-on-blue killings have called the principle of war by proxy into question.

Business alliances also have a long history.

Partnership as a means to commercialize technological advances was common long before James Watt linked his engineering genius to the entrepreneurial flair and managerial talents of Matthew Boulton in the 18th century in order to develop, manufacture and sell steam engines. In our own time, partnerships between inventive small firms and large companies with marketing and distribution clout were often seen as an alternative to licensing deals during the micro-electronics and micro-biology revolutions of the 1970s and 1980s. They are still regarded as a good way for small high-tech companies to reach overseas markets.

Partnership was the only way for large companies to enter overseas markets where majority local ownership was required by law. It was also seen as an effective way to respond to major plate-shifts in the world economy, such as the disintegration of the Soviet bloc,

European integration, the opening up of China and globalization in general.

Another partnership theme has been the replacement of conventional market-based relationships between suppliers and buyers with more intimate alliances. First seen as a cheaper and less risky way to exert control over the value chain than vertical integration, this model later developed into the 'value-adding partnership' (VAP): a group of independent companies working together to manage the flow of goods and services along their value chain. Some early American railroad firms resembled VAPs. The idea of the VAP survives in the modern VAR (value-added re-seller): a firm favoured by an original supplier, because it adds value to its products or services before selling them on.

The growth of business partnerships is both a symptom and a cause of the emergence of the VUCA environment: a symptom, because, in a VUCA world where politics and cross cultural tension can overwhelm economic calculations, partnerships are often the only way to grow internationally; a cause, because partnerships are less stable and controllable than integrated organizations.

A 1995 study by consultants Booz-Allen & Hamilton found that the number of joint ventures, licensing deals, collaborative research, exchanges of technology and marketing alliances had exploded over the previous decade. US companies had formed only 750 partnerships in the 1970s but were forming thousands per year in the mid-1990s as globalization was getting into its stride. The Booz-Allen study estimated that revenues from alliances in 1995 accounted for 6% of the revenues of America's 1,000 largest companies, as opposed to less than 2% in 1987. The study's authors concluded that 'a new chapter in the evolution of free enterprise' had begun.[3]

Another study by Andersen Consulting (now Accenture) in 1999 found that 82% of *Fortune 500* executives surveyed saw alliances as prime vehicles for growth: they accounted, on average, for 26% of *Fortune 500* members' revenues (up from 11% in 1994) and for 6-15% of their market value. Respondents expected alliances to account for 16-25% of their companies' market value within five years. But there were downside risks. The study found the 15 most successful alliances had created $72bn of shareholder value but the 15 least successful had destroyed $43bn of value.[4]

A 2003 study by consultants A. T. Kearney found the share prices of the best exponents of partnership (those with a long history of successful relationships) out-performed their industry peers by over 5% but those with poor records under-performed by nearly 12%.[5]

An analysis of mergers and Foreign Direct Investment (FDI) figures by KPMG in 2012 identified 220 joint ventures, worth $12.1bn, in emerging markets in 2011. This was slightly lower than the 2010 figure of $15.5bn, but was still the second highest total on record for emerging-market joint ventures and more than double the $5.2bn recorded in 2000. China was the favourite destination country once again as it had been in all but one year between 2004 and 2011. The KPMG analysis suggests that joint ventures accounted for about 17% of all FDI in emerging markets in 2011.[6]

Whatever the motivations for such alliances and partnerships, they all involve teaming up with other organizations or individuals not under your control whose objectives, although they seem compatible with yours at the time, aren't subordinate to yours. As with any type of alliance, there is always a risk that you will fall out with your partner or that your partner will turn against you.

Although pre-disposed to collaborate rather than control, the LFP organization does not eschew acquisitions altogether. Sometimes it will seem better, to both parties, to acquire a small company with interesting aptitudes or technology, than to collaborate with it. Disney collaborated with Pixar. Apple bought SoundJam (see Chapter 5). But in an LFP company, with its typical modular structure, the post-acquisition situation between acquirer and acquired will feel more like a partnership than a master-servant relationship.

Trust

The conventional wisdom about business partnerships is that if you trust too easily, you will be taken for a ride. You must make sure that you have a clear understanding of your prospective partner's interests, intentions and other relationships, insist on a bullet-proof partnership agreement and plan the divorce in detail before tying the knot.

In a VUCA world, that's a recipe for being left on the shelf. There is no time for lengthy partnership 'due diligence'. Opportunities for mutually beneficial partnerships appear today and may be gone tomorrow. If you insist on covering every angle and anticipating every eventuality, there is a good chance your prospective partner will look around for a less fastidious ally.

To use Francis Fukuyama's term LFP companies are inherently 'high-trust' organizations,[7] because their modular structures would not work without a relatively high degree of trust between modules and the centre. This habit of trusting 'insiders' translates into a predisposition to trust 'outsiders' such as customers, clients, suppliers and potential partners. The risks associated with this habit of trust are mitigated by the self-adjusting quality of each of the LFP company's modules. If a module trusts an organization or an individual initially and that trust is betrayed, the cheater is immediately cut out.

The general idea is that most people and most organizations can be trusted most of the time. Some partners may try to cheat you but if you are ready and able to cut them out as soon as they let you down, you can prevent them from doing much damage. The damage they do will be more than offset by the benefits of trust in your other relationships, which are substantial. Trustful relationships can be formed quickly and, once established, they operate more smoothly and efficiently than formal partnerships governed by minutely detailed processes, procedures and clauses covering irrelevant contractual undertakings.

The belief that a portfolio of informal partnerships based largely on trust will generate more value than a portfolio of more formal and intricately specified partnerships is corroborated by findings in game theory.

Corroboration of cooperation

Back in the early 1980s, game theorist Robert Axelrod organized a computer tournament designed to test decision rules submitted by other game theorists for an iterated version of a game known as the 'Prisoners' Dilemma'. He published the results in his book *The Evolution of Cooperation*.[8]

Two accomplices in a 'crime' are arrested, charged, imprisoned and interrogated separately. Each can either confess or protest his or her innocence. If one confesses, and so implicates the other, he or she will get a lighter sentence if the second pleads innocence. If both confess, both are convicted as charged and sentenced. If both plead innocence, the case cannot be proved and both receive a light sentence for a less serious offence. The dilemma is that innocence is the worst plea if the other confesses, but confession is a bad plea if the other confesses too.

The game can be represented as a matrix of possible outcomes as in the diagram below.

PLAYER A

		Cooperate	Defect
PLAYER B	Cooperate	Both get reward for mutual cooperation = 3	Temptation to defect and sucker's payoff A gets 5, B gets 0
	Defect	Sucker's payoff and temptation to defect A gets 0, B gets 5	Both get punishment for mutual defection = 1

In Axelrod's version there are two players and two available moves: 'cooperation' (pleading innocence) and 'defection' (confessing).

Each player knows if he or she defects (D) and the other confesses (C), he or she wins the maximum five points ('temptation' to defect [T] = 5) and the other gets nothing ('sucker's' payoff [S] = 0).

Each player also knows that if both choose C, both will score three points ('reward' for mutual cooperation [R] = 3); if both choose D, both will get a meagre one point ('punishment' for mutual defection [P] = 1).

Notice how the scores sum: mutual defection (both choose D) yields a total of two points; defection and cooperation (one chooses D and the other chooses C) yields five points; mutual cooperation (both choose C) yields six points.

Any arrangement that yields only positive scores is a positive-sum game. Axelrod's scoring defines another feature: there's a premium on cooperation. Many scoring arrangements will do this. Some would force cooperation by giving it an absolute premium over defection, thereby removing the dilemma, but in this case there is a conditional premium on defection, the condition being that the other player is a sucker (cooperates).

For each player, the 'expected' return (the average score from two possible outcomes) is twice as high for defection ($[5+1] / 2 = 3$), as it is for cooperation ($[3+0] / 2 = 1.5$). This means the best play for one iteration of the game is D. This is true even though each player knows the other will see the game in the same way and the chances of winning are, therefore, slim. Game theory requires the assumption that one's opponent will make his or her best move, which is D. Both players have to go for T ($=5$) knowing that in all likelihood both will end up with P ($=1$).

But suppose there is more than one iteration: suppose each player knows there will be many plays. That is often the case in business and is always the case in a business partnership. In this case, R (reward for mutual cooperation) becomes in theory very attractive, because a string of Rs (3s) is three times better than a string of Ps (1s). A Harvard Business School professor once told the author that you meet people three times in your life: one time you have the upper hand, one time it's even and one time the other has the upper hand. He said the sequence was unknown and the outcome of the three encounters will depend on the way you behave on the first encounter.

The difficulty is that, given the sucker's payoff, it is risky to initiate cooperation. You are virtually certain to be taken to the cleaners. You need some way of conveying to the other player your cooperative intent. Since the rules forbid off-game diplomacy, the only way to signal to the other player is through your moves.

The forced D of the single-play game is a signal of sorts: it says 'I'm no sucker'. But the language is limited. Signals become communicative only when the C move is introduced but, as we've seen, it is dangerous to be the first to cooperate.

The task in Axelrod's iterated version of the game is to develop a set of decision rules that in a finite series of moves in a series of iterations will convey to the other player your willingness to cooperate if he or she cooperates.

In business, each player is engaged in many series of games at once with employees, investors, customers, suppliers, competitors and collaborators. The company whose style of play conveys cooperative intent soonest, and thus elicits cooperation, has a good chance of emerging the overall winner.

Axelrod invited game theorists to enter sets of decision rules for a series of 200-move iterated prisoner's dilemma games to a round-robin computer tournament. Each rule set was to play one game with every other rule set. The winner would be the rule set that scored the highest overall points score.

'Surprisingly,' Axelrod reported, 'there is a single property which distinguishes the relatively high-scoring entries [15 entries were submitted to the first tournament] from the relatively low-scoring entries. This is the property of being nice, which is to say never being the first to defect.' The top 8 of the 15 entries were nice and none of the others were. The average scores of nice strategies ranged from 472 to 504 points. The best the 'nasties' could do was 401.

One nice entry had the dubious distinction of not winning a single game. It was the simplest of all and was christened 'tit for tat' (TFT). TFT cooperates on the first move and then repeats the other player's play in the previous move.

TFT never won a game: but it won the tournament.

Axelrod organized subsequent tournaments with many more entries and indefinite numbers of plays (the 200-move limit had inspired some tricky 'end-game' tactics in which he was not interested). TFT won again and again.

Axelrod attributed TFT's success to four qualities:

1. It is *nice*. By being never the first to defect, it maximizes its chances of hitting a long runs of Rs.
2. It is *retaliatory*. It hits back immediately if its opponent defects. It will lose against nasty rules but will make sure the price of its opponent's victory is a low score.
3. It is *forgiving*. TFT doesn't bear grudges. It will retaliate right away if its opponent defects but will cooperate again if its opponent cooperates. By not over-punishing it reduces the chances of a series of mutual-defection scores.
4. It is *clear*. Its simplicity makes it easily recognizable and since it tends to acquire a formidable reputation, it should quickly elicit cooperation.

These four qualities fit the picture of the LFP organization being developed here like the proverbial glove.

The LFP organization is 'high trust': it has a propensity to trust both internally and externally. Axelrod would call it 'nice'.

The LFP organization and its modules are self-adjusting: they will do unto others what others do to them. It is 'retaliatory'.

Its trust, once lost, can be regained, if its betrayer is contrite and demonstrates its penitence. LFP companies are 'forgiving'.

The LFP organization is consistent in its treatment of others and earns a reputation for being nice, retaliatory and forgiving. It's 'clear'. In modern parlance, the LFP organization will acquire the equivalent of a 'four star' rating on eBay.

Collaboration as a *leitmotiv*

The shape of the modern company is said by economists to have been deeply influenced by 'transaction costs', of which there are three main types:

1. *Search and information* costs incurred in finding the required goods or services with the lowest price.
2. *Bargaining costs* incurred while reaching an agreement with the other party to the transaction, drawing up appropriate contracts, etc . . .
3. *Policing and enforcement costs* incurred while ensuring the other party sticks to the terms of the contract.

Ronald Coase argued that integrated firms had evolved, because, by suppressing the internal price system, they saved the 'transaction costs' that arose when markets balanced supply and demand.[9]

Coase's ideas were later developed into a broad theory of the firm by his former student, Oliver Williamson, winner of the 2009 Nobel Prize for economics. According to Williamson, the modern company is 'the product of a series of organizational innovations that have had the purpose and effect of economizing on transaction costs'.[10] He says transaction costs can be very substantial, because people are opportunistic but not omniscient, and tend to act in a 'boundedly rational', rather than a purely rational way.[11]

Williamson acknowledged that the reduction in transaction costs in an integrated organization must be set against the growing 'agency costs' of management – the imperfect matching of supply and demand and the tendency of managers to pursue their own ends (as did the English East India Company's *nabobs*; see Chapter 1) at the expense of shareholders as the organization grows. He saw the multi-unit company as a solution to this problem, because its scale captured transaction cost economies, and the independence of profit centres controlled agency costs.In his book, *The Visible Hand*,[12] Alfred Chandler suggested that 'multi-unit business enterprises' (MUBEs) replaced the traditional single-unit enterprise when:

- The routinizing of transactions reduced transaction costs.
- The linking of the administration of producing, buying and distributing units reduced information costs.
- The internalization of many units permitted the administrative co-ordination of flows of goods between units, leading to more effective scheduling, more intensive use of facilities and personnel, increased productivity, lower costs, more certain cash flow and faster payment.

The conventional wisdom, therefore, is that large integrated firms evolved because they balanced supply and demand more cheaply than the market.

But suppose there were no transaction costs. Modern technology, particularly the Internet (search engines, price comparison sites and online auctions), have reduced 'search and information' costs substantially. And the 'high-trust' LFP company incurs much lower bargaining, policing and enforcement costs than a conventional organization. Will this encourage the emergence of less integrated organizations? If Chandler's MUBE was, as Coase suggested, invoked by the superiority, in the mid-19th century, of administrative over market coordination of business activities, could the reversal of this balance of advantage invoke another, more collaborative, less integrated kind of organization?

It could even be argued that in the special case of partnership v. acquisition, the transaction costs associated with the former could actually be negative. This possibility arises because a company or an individual might be willing to deliver more value per dollar as a partner than as a subsidiary or an employee. As discussed, the enthusiasm with which we have contributed, for free, vast amounts of knowledge and information to Wikipedia, demonstrates the enormous productive potential lying latent in the passions and enthusiasms of ordinary people.

As transaction costs fall, the economics of collaboration relative to integration will improve and forming partnerships will become a better and cheaper way to assemble the components of value chains. In time, communities of like-minded high-trust LFP companies could emerge in which transaction costs are close to zero.

ARM Holdings

Acorn Computers designed the world's first commercial, single-chip RISC (Reduced Instruction Set Computer) in 1985 and used it in its Archimedes computer, launched in 1987.

But Acorn, based in Cambridge in the UK, knew the potential market for its fast, energy-efficient chips, which were easy to program and had good code density (they needed less memory than competing RISCs), extended way beyond personal computers. In an effort to tap the wider market, the company 'spun out' the RISC development team in November 1990 to form Advanced RISC Machines (ARM).

The traditional way to exploit such a lead is to raise a bundle of money and set up an integrated, design, development, manufacturing and marketing business. When Robin Saxby (now Sir Robin) was being interviewed for the job of ARM's CEO he proposed another approach. 'My idea was to run lean and quickly, and get into profit fast. We had outstanding people, a leading architecture and the chance to transform it from an Acorn, into a global standard. But we did not have the capital for manufacturing.'[13]

Saxby saw ARM's *raison d'être* as designing and developing advanced RISC processors and systems. ARM would stick to that. Everything else needed to make ARM's chips world beaters would be provided by what Saxby called 'partnering in multiple dimensions'. ARM did not form partnerships from time to time as expediency dictated. It was built on them. 'That's the benefit of a clean sheet of paper,' said Saxby. 'We had no history so we could plan for [partnerships] from the outset and concentrate on doing what we were best at.'

ARM licenses its designs to its partners, who manufacture, develop applications for and market their products. 'We can licence to anyone we want,' said Saxby. 'We charge an up-front licence fee and then a royalty per piece.' One important attraction for ARM's partners is that ARM's multiple partnerships make it easy for them to arrange local sources of supply. Another attraction is the ARM practice of publishing its product development plans, or 'roadmaps', as Saxby called them. This allowed ARM's partners to plan their own product development around specifications for more advanced chips that ARM had committed itself to developing.

The roadmaps exemplified ARM's partnering philosophy because they revealed to partners product development plans that a conventional semiconductor company would have regarded as highly confidential. Saxby saw it differently. He wanted ARM's partners to commit long-term to the ARM architecture. To be willing to do that, they would need, he believed, to know what ARM was planning. 'It costs us and our semiconductor partners, several million dollars to develop a new chip . . . we have to be sure there are products ready and waiting for it.'

ARM's research and development is also based on partnerships with universities and other research institutions. As Saxby put it, 'we re-cycle intellectual property'. ARM was part of what Saxby called the 'Cambridge keretsu'; an autocatalytic network of academic and business people, which spawned ARM's parent, Acorn, and many other high-tech firms that have sprung up around the university town.

By 1997, Saxby was happy with the results of the business model he had proposed at his interview six years earlier. Sales had risen from less than £1m in 1991 to £10m in 1995 and, following start-up losses, operating profits had reached £3m. 'It seems to work in the early stages, at least. We are self-funding and cash generating.' Sales and profits were £42m and £9m respectively in 1998, the year ARM's shares were listed on the London and NASDAQ stock exchanges. Saxby retired as chairman in 2006 leaving ARM in rude health. In the year to December 31 2011, ARM's 2,116 full-time employees had generated revenues of £492m and pre-tax profits of £230m.

Commenting on the 2011 results on January 31 2012, ARM CEO Warren East said the company: 'has seen strong licensing growth, driven by market-leading semiconductor companies increasing their commitment to ARM technology, and more new customers choosing ARM technology for the first time. We have also seen our royalty revenue continue to grow faster than industry revenues.' He predicted that revenues for 2012 would 'be at least in line with' the market's expectation of just over $860m (£537.5m).

ARM's strategy, if one can call it that, is indistinguishable from its partnership business model. In effect, it borrows its strategy from its partners. It is part of several distributed enterprises in several markets and its fate is the fate of all its partners. ARM sees itself and its partners as members of a community. It claimed in a press release issued in February 2009, for example, that the fact that over 60 'ARM Connected Community' members would be show-casing ARM technology at the forthcoming Mobile World Congress in Barcelona demonstrated 'the impressive strength and growth of the ARM ecosystem'.

ARM sees each partnership as long-term. It has no idea of where it will lead. It's content to take one step at a time. Its people are inspired by faith in the RISC technology they have mastered. They go where it leads. They have no desire to plan its life in detail. They're great project planners, but they have no 'strategy' in the conventional sense of the word.

Secrecy

One advantage of treading lightly is that others, including rivals and competitors, might not hear you coming. If you keep your plans under your hat and move quietly on tip-toe, you could take them by surprise and win the battle, or the competition, before they guess your intentions.

All three elements of President Obama's 'light footprint' warfare doctrine rely to some extent on the element of surprise. If the targets of combat drones hear the machines coming, they can make themselves scarce. If word of Stuxnet, and of its appetite for Siemens software, had got out, the engineers at the Natanz enrichment facility could have erected barriers against the malware. If Osama bin Laden's spies had heard whispers about Operation Neptune Spear on the grapevine, and knew when the SEALs planned to strike, he could have left the compound in Abbottabad or made arrangements that would have frustrated the raid (see Chapter 2).

LFP companies are the just same, because they know that if no hint of their intentions leaks out before they act, they can accomplish much more, with much less. If Sheila Regan's competitors in her target Latin American city had known about her 'Operation Hit Back', they could have countered the move and would not have been misled into thinking the competition was too strong (see Chapter 5).

Secrecy, high security, surreptitious preparation, small groups of people who keep their mouths shut – all are essential elements of the LFP approach. LFP companies may not have detailed strategies or battle plans that a rival can steal or hack into, but tactical hit-and-run raids take a lot of detailed planning and it may require several practice runs to get the all-important timing right.

These days 'transparency' is deemed to be a virtue and secrecy is regarded as, if not a vice in itself, a cloak beneath which vices may go undetected. Conventional companies tend to be 'transparent' for two reasons: first, because they want everything they do to be seen to be above board and fully compliant with laws, regulations and ethical norms; second, because they want employees to 'buy in' to their plans and investment analysts to base their calculations of the company's value on its plans, as well as on its record.

It may sometimes be difficult for LFP companies to comply with the demand for 'transparency' of all kinds. This may make it hard for employees to 'buy in' to plans and have a sense of direction and for investment analysts to judge the value of the LFP company: at least initially, before the company has had a chance to demonstrate the strength of the LFP approach and its ability to create value.

This is why the LFP organization's vision needs to be revealed and its brand identity needs to be deliberately cultivated. 'We can't tell you what we're going to do,' the LFP company tells its various constituencies (its existing and prospective employees, investors, customers, partners and suppliers) 'but we will do all that we can to show you what we are'.

That's the original meaning of 'strategy': a leader with a vision and a well-trained, well-equipped, multi-competent army.

Collateral damage

A consequence of Obama's substitution of 'light footprint' warfare for the Powell doctrine of overwhelming force is that the American people have become much more aware of the body-bag count.

When land armies confronted each other large numbers of casualties were expected. During the battle of the Somme, between July 1 and November 18 1916, over 300,000 combatants were killed and 800,000 were injured. The carnage was horrifying but not surprising. Death was the currency of war. A bloodless victory was inconceivable. Although regrettable, non-combatant casualties (collateral damage) were seen as the unavoidable price that had to be paid for victory in 'total war'.

In the age of precision-guided munitions, UAVs and special forces, each non-combatant death is seen by ordinary people as an error: a failure of command or of equipment. There is much less collateral damage in light footprint warfare of course, but the non-combatant deaths, particularly of children, that do occur are felt that much more keenly and when they are reported in the media, they tend to cause more reputational damage.

The Obama administration's sensitivity to non-combatant casualties in covert drone strikes is reported to have led to a re-definition of 'combatants' as all males of military age in the strike zone if there is no explicit posthumous intelligence to the contrary.

The outbreak of hostilities between Israel, among the world's most technologically advanced military nations, and poorly armed gunmen and rocket squads in Hamas-controlled Gaza in November 2012, could hardly have been more of a mismatch. But as Shlomo Brom, a retired Israeli general, put it. 'This is the kind of encounter that can't end with a knockout . . . there are no victories in these conflicts.'

Yiftah Shapir of the Institute of National Security Studies in Tel Aviv called the confrontation, 'a classic example of asymmetric warfare . . . [It] takes place not on the ground but on TV and computer screens all over the world'.[14]

Although seldom decisive, media relations and brand management are as vital for business in the VUCA world as they are for warfare.

A new species

The LFP company has a distinctive presence in the business world.

It's light, alert and quick on its feet. It's highly automated and cyber-savvy. It prefers raids to frontal attacks. It is extremely centralized, but extremely decentralized too. It is promiscuous in its eagerness to form new partnerships, but those who try to take advantage of its apparently naïve readiness to trust, quickly find that it retaliates instantly, if crossed. It plays its cards close to its chest. It cares about the consequences of its actions.

To the outsider, it looks like a new species: smart, unpredictable and as slippery as quicksilver. Worth keeping a close eye on, but that's easier said than done. It moves like a dragonfly: hovers, darts suddenly, hovers again. It is hard for predators and prey to keep track of it.

If that's what an LFP company looks like to an outsider, what does it look like to an insider? That's the question to be addressed in the next chapter.

---

[1] Times Books, 2002.

[2] 'Orpheus Chamber Orchestra Embodies Democratic Principles: Self-governing Orchestra Empowers Musicians': *Axiom News*, October 28, 2008.

[3] *A Practical Guide to Alliances*: Booz-Allen & Hamilton, 1995.

[4] Cited in: *Strategic Alliances: The Right Way to Compete in the 21st Century*: Ivey Business Journal, September/October 2001.

[5] *The Partnering Imperative: Making Business Partnerships Work:* John Wiley, 2003.

[6] *Joint ventures on the rise*: KPMG, 2012.

[7] *Trust: The Social Virtues and the Creation of Prosperity*: The Free Press, 1995.

[8] *The Evolution of Cooperation*: Basic Books, 1984.

[9] 'The Nature of the Firm': *Economica*, 1937.

[10] 'The Modern Corporation: Origins, Evolution, Attributes': *Journal of Economic Literature*, 1981.

[11] 'The Economics of Organization: The Transaction Cost Approach': *American Journal of Sociology*, 1981.

[12] *The Visible Hand: The Managerial Revolution in American Business*: Harvard University Press, 1977.

[13] *The Partnering Imperative: op cit.*

[14] 'Clear-cut victory set to elude Israel and Hamas': *Financial Times*, November 21, 2012.

Chapter 7

The LFP organization

Company leaders trying to make their organizations more agile, and thus better adapted to a VUCA environment, are wrestling with the same challenge that confronted the designers of combat aircraft in the 1980s.

The fighter plane designers arrived at what seemed at that time to be a counter-intuitive solution. Because they saw stability as the enemy of agility, they designed the new generation of 'agile combat aircraft' (ACA) to be aerodynamically unstable.

The same search for the edge of stability, where agility is at its maximum, occurs in Formula 1 motor racing. The greatest F1 drivers configure their cars (tyre pressures, wing settings, spring rates, ride height, etc.) so close to the edge of instability that lesser drivers would be off the track at the first corner.

But though they fly in unstable configurations, ACAs are not often unstable. They contrive artificial stability through the control of their moving surfaces by sensors and flight computers, which are constantly detecting and correcting departures from the chosen equilibrium.

Because this 'fly-by-wire' arrangement is mission critical (if the flight control system 'crashes', the plane's unstable aerodynamics become instantly and catastrophically obvious), ACA flight control systems are at least triplex and often quadruplex.

The value of an aerodynamically unstable configuration is not that it allows higher 'g' (gravity) in turns but that it allows faster rates of change in 'g'. A stable airframe can pull as much 'g' as an unstable airframe but it can't handle such rapid increases and decreases in 'g'.

The main constraint in ACA design is what an ACA designer calls 'a poorly-defined government-provided piece of equipment', namely the pilot. The ability of human pilots to handle 'g', rates of change in 'g' and other departures from normal, life-supporting conditions, imposes limits on flight performance way below what is technically possible. As the designer said, from an engineer's point of view, a human pilot 'is the worst possible mix of frailties'.

An ACA's life support system is not just a set of sub-systems that maintains a chemically and thermally habitable cockpit. It is also a set of constraints: a dynamic envelope beyond which the aircraft cannot stray, without risking the impairment of its human pilot's effectiveness. To put it another way, the 'software' (in the flight control computers) must never instruct the 'hardware' (the ACA) to behave in ways that incapacitate the 'wetware' (the pilot).

Agile drones (remote-controlled, or autonomous) can be designed to be much more agile than ACAs.

The corollary for companies is clear. If the organization is to be sufficiently agile to thrive in a VUCA world, it must be close to the edge of uncontrollability. Or, to put it in the terms used by complexity scientists, it must try to occupy the 'chaotic' region between stability and instability where creativity and novelty are maximized.

But it's not as simple to implement as it is to describe.

As the ACA's 'wetware' constraints suggest, there are human limits to the scale and rate of change an organization can tolerate. Over time people get used to change. It becomes 'normal'. This acquired tolerance allows performance limits to be pushed higher. But there will always be limits beyond which the organization collapses into hopeless disorganization.

Balanced

VUCA-adapted LFP organizations are constantly seeking these 'sweet spots' between opposites.

Hope and fear

Organizations trying to adapt to the VUCA world must find and then maintain a balance between hope and fear, if the organization is not either to collapse into hopeless disorganization or revert to a more stable, but less agile state.

This trade-off between stability and agility means that the search for agility is risky. Stabilities that were previously supplied by tight control and discipline have to be abandoned and replaced by peer pressure, self-organization and the equivalents of triplex or quadruplex flight control systems in ACAs, such as culture, values and vision.

Trust, horizontal, between peers and vertical, between management levels, is essential in a VUCA-adapted organization.

Friendship, watching each other's back, and a sense of reciprocal obligation all contribute to the self-organization that allows the system to be under control when no-one is in control. Comradeship is the glue that binds together members of a special forces unit and gives to each the confidence to put his life in his comrades' hands. It is common in small start-up companies, but tends to fade away as a company grows and becomes more complex and as employees become more narrowly specialized.

One of the advantages of the modular organization is that the glue of comradeship re-appears within the modules.

Vertical trust between levels (e.g., fair or due process, ownership and 'empowerment') is required to maintain the appropriate balance between fear and hope. When fear is the dominant emotion, the group tends to be stable but to lack creativity and adaptability. But a certain amount of fear is also needed. The group must be deterred, by its anxieties, from some courses of action, and also driven, by its hopes, towards others.

As Schwenker and Müller-Dofel have pointed out (see Chapter 3), the company leader has a responsibility to allay fear and give people a sense of security. Authenticity and consistency are crucial when building trust in the vertical plane. The leader has a role, but must not play a role. He or she must be and must be seen to be the same person in every situation.

Leaders must allay many kinds of fear. Technophobia is one example of potentially debilitating fear. IT is advancing so rapidly these days that some people, particularly older people less comfortable with new technologies, such as 'smart' phones, that younger people take for granted, can be left behind and feel disenfranchized. They will have important contributions to make in other areas that could be lost if their technophobia is allowed to disempower them.

Change and continuity

As much as some would like to, leaders can't re-invent, re-design or re-make the organizations in their charge. An organization is what it is. It has history, memories, a legacy, a culture and a brand. It is much more than an abstraction – much more than a place where people do and are done by.

Numbers tell us something about organizations, but they are always out of date, frequently misleading and irredeemably monochrome. They tell us nothing about what organizations look, feel and smell like.

Much richer information is provided by stories about relationships and encounters with organizations told by those who work, or have worked in them, and those outside them whose lives are or have been touched by them in one way or another.

The crucial difference between stories told in numbers and stories told in words is that the former focus on differences and on what changes, while the latter focus on similarities and on what stays the same. Numbers have meaning only insofar as they differ from the numbers relating to other times, or other businesses. Stories told in words may be about change, or a series of changes, but are held together in narratives by what stays the same despite change.

In VUCA times, managers must understand what stays the same despite change because without anchors that connect what was, what is and what will be to what endures, people find it hard to adapt to new circumstances and respond to new challenges.

The word 'brand' is usually used to describe distinctive qualities a company's customers associate with its products or services. But the company has other 'brands', or distillations of reputations or perceptions, that lodge in the minds of its employees, suppliers, partners and competitors. In essence, all brands are memories that stay more or less the same, or that change only slowly. The founders of companies lay the foundations of their distinctive identities and the brands they carry with them through time.

Steve Jobs, the co-founder of Apple, expressed something about the enduring but evolving Apple brand when he said, 'simplicity is the ultimate sophistication'.

Managers of large, listed companies must nurture these brands and recognize that they don't own the organizations they lead. They're stewards for a while. The true essence of companies existed before they arrived and, if they make no disastrous mistakes, the essence will remain more or less the same after they're gone. They need to keep in mind the original intent of the company's founder and the 'ultimate mission', such as the over-arcting 'Protect America' mission of the US Army.

Vertical and horizontal

During the early years of the hunt for Osama bin Laden, the Central Intelligence Agency (CIA) was continually frustrated. Robert Fry suggested that this might have been because: 'the regimented structures of Soviet governance or the Iraqi Republican Guard had habituated CIA analysts to expect form, hierarchy and structure amongst its enemies, characteristics conspicuously absent in al Qaeda. The organization had always been loose and organic . . . While the CIA continued to seek vertical patterns of organization, al Qaeda conducted its operations by horizontal proliferation of its command. But, as time went on, the CIA became more flexible in its approach and eventually . . . got lucky.'[1]

There is vertical form and structure throughout the VUCA world, of course, particularly in large companies. But there is also a great deal of horizontal form and structure, which tends to be harder to spot for companies 'habituated' like the CIA analysts '. . . to expect form, hierarchy and structure' amongst its competitors.

Soon after its launch in 1981, IBM's personal computer (PC) came to dominate the market. By the end of the decade it was a relatively minor player. It sold its PC division and the ThinkPad PC brand to the Chinese company, Lenovo, for $1.25bn in 2005. But Big Blue's PC business wasn't brought to its knees in the late 1980s by stronger or better-led competitors. It was humbled by a chain of horizontal business relationships between what were, at that time, relatively small companies (Microsoft, Intel, Compaq, Dell) each pursuing its own goals. Together, they comprised a powerful business enterprise IBM failed to spot because it had no recognizable, vertical shape or threatening intent.

In the VUCA world, opportunities, threats and novelty emerge mostly from the horizontal plane, from the spaces between businesses, as opposed to these within businesses. The spaces between businesses have always been important sources of novelty, but there are many of them in a VUCA setting; the dramatic reductions in transaction costs in recent years have reduced the costs of market coordination, relative to those of 'administrative' coordination (see Chapter 6).

The individual and the organization

From time to time, the management literature turns its attention to political and constitutional issues. There has been talk over the years of 'empowerment', the 'psychological contract', the rights and duties of employees and the prerogatives, responsibilities and privileges of managers and leaders, of the basis, distribution and assignment of power, of distributive justice and fair rewards.

In a VUCA world, attention must be paid to such matters because an organization that can keep its balance in a volatile, uncertain, complex and ambiguous business environment is very different from one adapted to a stable environment.

With unmanageable complexity, the actions of individuals cannot be prescribed in detail. All managers can do is create a framework in which the group's self-organising qualities are guided by a shared sense of fate.

LFP organizations are modular rather than integrated. They consist of small, well-trained, well-equipped, agile, flexible and largely self-managing teams or groups (see Chapter 5).

The conjecture that 'modular' organizations are more adaptable and better-equipped to prosper in the VUCA environment is corroborated by the findings of complexity scientists. They have shown that, in a stable and predictable environment, an integrated, ordered system is better at solving problems but that in unstable, unpredictable environments problem-solving by small, independent units, none of which is 'minding the whole store', out-performs centralized problem-solving for the benefit of the whole system. This suggests modular non-hierarchical structures, in which each module is autonomous and self-governing, produce better results.

This has important implications for leadership in LFP, VUCA-adapted organizations. 'Control freaks', and those who believe in the need for a 'central command' management style, need not apply.

A modular structure also has valuable defensive qualities in fifth domain competition. When each module has its own closed management system (are we entering a post-ERP era?), the whole organization is less vulnerable to cyber weapon attacks.

The challenge for leaders of modular, LFP organizations is that, in such organizations, there is less need for conventional leadership because the modules manage themselves and the interactions between them rely on the self-organizing qualities of complex systems. The two crucial principles for managing LFP organizations are to take great care when allocating resources (see Chapter 8) and to cultivate a culture in which the modules feel empowered to manage themselves without interference. The leader must trust each module to make the right decisions.

As the Daoist sage Lao Tzu said, 'When the best leader's work is done the people say, "We did it ourselves"'.

The 'real' organization

In the pre-VUCA environment, and with the pre-LFP company, there are two organizations: the 'ideal' organization, which is the one best equipped to realize the leader's strategic intent, and the organization as it really is. In pre-LFP organizations most change programmes are designed to bring the 'real' organization closer to the 'ideal', so that the leader's strategic intent is more likely to come to fruition. In LFP organizations, change programmes are still required from time to time, but are designed to improve the real organization. They are pragmatic, rather than idealistic.

Change programmes in LFP organizations are more successful than in strategy-led organizations for two reasons: they are less ambitious – initially, at any rate – and they treat the real organization with more respect as a living organism in a particular state, which can improve and heal itself.

To improve the real organization or module, it's first necessary to understand it. The Japanese idea of 'Gemba', the 'real place', urges managers who want to know what's going on to go to the place where it is going on, and then to watch and listen.

This is the organization's musculature and cellular structure, the main repository of its skills, abilities, knowledge, and wisdom.

Isao Endo, Chairman of Roland Berger (Japan), and Professor at the Graduate School of Asia-Pacific Studies, Waseda University, calls it 'Gemba Power' and warns that company leaders who try to change their organizations without taking it into account are asking for trouble.

He says that, in their efforts to cope with the 'triple handicap of overcapacity, superfluous personnel and excess debt', most Japanese companies tightened their belts and down-sized 'haphazardly', only to find they had: 'lost the Gemba ideology and wisdom traditionally passed from generation to generation'. As a result, the 'workplace . . . stopped thinking deeply.'[2]

Endo argues that profitability, stock price, customer satisfaction and brand value are output measures and 'nothing more than shadows revealed when a light is shone on the corporation'. He says that a 'strong company' has a competitive strategy/vision, the ability to implement the strategy 'nimbly, efficiently and effectively' (this is 'Gemba Power'), and leadership that forges strong links between the vision and 'Gemba Power'.

According to Endo, Gemba is the corporate engine-room, where value is created. The role of head-office and management is to support the Gemba. This turns the conventional view, which sees operations as subservient to head office and management, upside down.

Gemba Power is autonomous and active in that it addresses problems spontaneously when they arise. It's synergistic in that it emerges from

– and is greater than – the sum of the individuals involved. It's wise, in the sense that it thinks deeply. Like the *esprit de corps* in the military's special forces, it emerges from friendships and the acknowledgement of reciprocal obligations in the workplace.

Gemba is based on teamwork and acts horizontally through what Endo calls 'operational chains' and combinations of operational chains. 'For horizontally linked operations to go smoothly,' he says, 'those involved in the chain must not only be responsible for their own work, but also be aware of the quality of the entire chain. "Gemba Power" strengthens the . . . operational chain, which if left alone may break or become only partially optimized.'

In Endo's view, the competitive advantage conferred by Gemba Power is far greater and more durable than that conferred by a strategic advantage, the lifespan of which 'is significantly shorter than we tend to think'.

Self-organizing

Although he doesn't use the term, Endo implies that Gemba Power is self-organizing in at least two ways.

The first is that in its constant quest for operational efficiency it automatically seeks out and removes waste, inconsistencies and physical strains (*muda, mura, muri*) in the operational chains, and so achieves 'a smooth and continuous work flow'.

The second is that Gemba is not, as 'operations' are often seen to be, an internal, introspective set of activities pre-occupied with its own affairs. On the contrary, through operational chains that extend beyond the borders of the business, it senses customer needs and wants and is interested in their implications for possible new products and services. As Endo puts it, 'A strong Gemba is like an antenna that is sensitive to these seeds of new customer value'.

Gemba is the essence of the company. Its muscles move the business and its eyes and ears sense the best direction for that movement. If management can resist the temptation to confine it within its conventional 'silo' under the control of a Chief Operating Officer, it can, through its natural propensity to organize itself, greatly increase the company's efficiency, flexibility and adaptability.

These are the qualities required in a VUCA world and they are more likely to emerge from less top-down management than more top-down management. This doesn't mean that leadership is superfluous in an LFP organization. It means that LFP organizations need a different kind of leadership and needs leaders with different qualities (see Chapter 9).

Data friendly

US intelligence spending has traditionally been classified but, in 2007, the government began to lift the veil of secrecy by revealing the National Intelligence Program (NIP) budget. This is one of the two components of the overall budget for the 16 agencies of the US Intelligence Community and is under the control of the Director of National Intelligence (DNI). It covers all intelligence activities apart from those related to military operations. These are covered by the Military Intelligence Program (MIP) budget.

In October 2010, the DNI, Dennis Blair, revealed that the aggregate amount appropriated by Congress to the NIP for the year to the end of September 2010 was $53.1bn. The MIP budget for the same period, revealed for the first time in 12 years, was $27bn.

The total Intelligence Community budget of $80.1bn was three times as much as when the total was last disclosed, in response to a lawsuit, in 1998. It compared with annual budgets of $53bn and $30bn for the US Department of Homeland Security and the Justice Department respectively and with a total defence budget of $664bn.

It can be inferred from these figures that the US military believe that, in a VUCA world, you need to spend roughly an eighth of your total budget on gathering and analyzing information.

Whether this is also the right proportion for a company in the new VUCA world is impossible to say. It will depend on the company and its particular circumstances. It is certainly true, however, that every LFP company takes the gathering and analysis of information very seriously and devotes considerable resources to it. There is no point in being agile and fast if your antenna and other sensors are insufficiently sensitive to pick up the faint signals from the environment that herald opportunities and threats.

The ability to pick up weak signals derived from the gathering and analysis of information is essential because, in a competitive and fast-changing marketplace, you have to act first. If you wait until the case for action is overwhelming, you will act too late.

But in the cacophony of the cloud, how can the organization decide which weak signals to heed?

One of the great ironies of the VUCA world is that it's awash with so much data that it can be extremely hard to find unequivocal information on which to base decisions.

There was a time when knowledge was power: when the authority of a leader was derived, partly at any rate, from his or her privileged access to important information. Now everyone knows or can know, if he or she chooses, practically anything.

The poison is in the dose, as Paracelsus said. When information is scarce, every titbit of data is of value. When we're all inundated with it, and most of it is garbage, it can become a distraction, a source of friction and distrust that undermines relationships. And it can lead to indecisive leadership.

It's like carbon dioxide: if there's too little, we have no plants and we can't survive; if there's too much, there's rampant global warming and we can't survive.

From being an invaluable resource, data have become a pollutant and are generating more heat than light. The 'experts' we used to rely on have become less dependable because there are too many of them now, saying different things.

Companies have learned, over the past few decades or so, to become environmentally friendly. One of the major challenges for managers in the VUCA world is to become 'data friendly' in two senses: they need to be capable of extracting commercially valuable information from the rivers of data constantly flowing through them and around them, and they need to be capable of quickly distilling the rivers of data into the relevant, 'to-the-point' information that leaders at every level require in order to make well-informed and timely decisions.

Mining 'big data'

It will not be enough to develop ever more sophisticated knowledge management systems. 'Data friendliness' in the VUCA world requires an acknowledgement of the possibility that the persistent validity of 'Moore's Law' (promulgated by Intel co-founder Gordon Moore in 1965), which says the number of transistors on integrated circuits doubles every two years, is bringing us to a phase transition – namely to a critical point beyond which business changes fundamentally.

Björn Bloching, Lars Luck and Thomas Ramge explain the approaching event horizon (comparable to the 'singularity point' in Artificial Intelligence research noted in Chapter 5) in their book, *In Data We Trust*: 'Data storage is becoming ever cheaper, data processing ever faster and the algorithmic software that analyses the data is ever more intelligent. Information scientists have dubbed this revolution "Big Data". Big Data will change society, politics, and business as fundamentally as electricity and the Internet.'[3]

But haven't we heard it all before in the late 1990s? All the talk about Customer Relationship Management (CRM), data mining, loyalty cards and segment-of-one marketing? After the dot.com bubble burst in 2001, interest in CRM declined. As Bloching, Luck and Ramge put it: 'CRM had turned from a magic word into a curse. Too many companies had set up too many data cemeteries – and buried too much money there . . . One of the most common [mistakes] derives from the attitude that the first thing to do is to collect lots of data . . . and then see what to do with it. That is a sure path to data overkill.' As the philosopher of science, the late Sir Karl Popper pointed out, you cannot simply 'observe'. You need to begin with a conjecture: with an idea of what you are looking for.

But although the initial enthusiasm for the new often gives way to disappointment and disenchantment, it doesn't always mean that the enthusiasm was mistaken. It may simply mean it was premature. The enthusiasm for 'dot.com' stocks in the late 90s was inspired by a belief that the Internet was a vast new domain for enterprise with enormous value creation potential. As the subsequent successes of companies such as Amazon, Google, eBay and Facebook have shown, the investors who fuelled the 'dot.com' boom lost bundles of money not because they were deluded but because they got the timing wrong.

Bloching *et al* argue that we are now on the threshold of realizing that premature belief.

They corroborate the prediction by describing Dirk Helbing's 'Live Earth Simulator' (LES), the prototypical machine of the 'big data' age. Helbing is building the machine at the science and technology university, ETH Zurich. He hopes to be able to use it to calculate the epidemic vector of a flu virus through the real-time analysis of incoming data, to identify effective measures to combat climate change, and to set off alarm bells if another financial crisis is looming. In business, the LES might be able to calculate whether a new product will make life difficult for the competition or simply cannibalize sales from the company's other products.

The LES has been described as the most ambitious divination system since the Oracle at Delphi. But it is not a machine for predicting the future. In the VUCA world, the future is non-deterministic and thus inherently unpredictable. (The Chinese understand this. Guided by the *I Ching*, they focus on movement itself rather than its end state, because they know that, if they can spot the movement early enough, they may be able to influence it.)

The LES deals with 'data', which is the plural of 'datum', meaning 'a given'. Note the past tense. The LES is an ultra-sophisticated data-mining machine. Its appearance of prescience is derived from the ability of its algorithms to spot connections between already recorded data ('givens') that are invisible to the human analyst's eye.

A machine that knows everything there is to know can't predict the unpredictable future but it can paint a probabilistic picture of the future likely to be much more accurate than anything we could paint unaided. As Bloching *et al* put it: 'Computers know us better than we know ourselves . . . [they are] often more reliable than we are at saying how we will behave in certain situations.'

Companies are already using 'big data' to reveal patterns of store congestion and the movement of people. Mining it can also help companies to know the minds of their competitors better than they know themselves.

In a statement to the press in February 2002, Donald Rumsfeld, the then US Secretary of Defense, and the chief architect of the light foot-print approach to warfare subsequently adopted and developed by President Obama, said:

> [T]here are known knowns; there are things we know that we know.
>
> There are known unknowns; that is to say there are things that we now know we don't know.
>
> But there are also unknown unknowns – there are things we do not know we don't know.

In the age of 'big data', machines such as Helbing's LES can help to turn known unknowns into known knowns. They can sometimes pick up unknown unknowns and turn them into known unknowns or even into known knowns. They can extrapolate and infer from what is known and in so doing, make some unknowns knowable. In other words they can eliminate unforced errors that stem from ignorance of what is or could have been known. But they cannot turn into knowns what is inherently unknowable.

When the work of 'big data' is done, the essence of VUCA remains.

Extracting 'little data'

'Big data' is one thing. Timely and pertinent information that helps decision-makers avoid unforced errors is another.

This is a major challenge for two reasons.

First, in a VUCA world, it may be very hard to distinguish between the relevant and irrelevant, the trivial and non-trivial, the odd jewel and the dross in the constant flow of data. When spilling a cup of coffee one winter afternoon can lead, through a sequence of steps no-one could have foreseen, to a company's insolvency seven months later, how can the decision-maker know what to look for, or what weight to attach to different pieces of information?

Second, in a VUCA world, it is vital to decide quickly. Windows of opportunity may not stay open long. Possible threats may turn into real and present dangers in the blink of an eye.

You can seldom 'know for sure' in a VUCA world. You can only 'know to best of your knowledge' LFP companies and their modules/teams are preternaturally curious and inquisitive because they want the best of their knowledge to be as good as it can possibly be. They invest considerable sums in gathering and analysing information. Their high gain antennae, as Isao Endo calls them (see above), are finely tuned and quiver with alertness.

Like Chinese company leaders who watch and listen intently to what is going on around them, they have an epistemology, an idea of what it is to 'know' in the VUCA world. Although they know they cannot know anything for sure, they know the kind of hints and clues that presage change or opportunity. They edit, prioritize, authenticate and interpret almost without thinking.

They are particularly interested in weak signals, like the Chinese entrepreneurs who read changes in politburo 'protocol rankings' in orders of mention in the state-owned media and seating positions in pictures of politburo meetings. High-velocity LFP organizations operating in fast changing environments heed the weak signals that presage opportunities or threats because they know that, if they wait until the signals are loud enough to be conclusive, they will have waited too long.

This has two practical implications for synthesizing and reporting information. The leader needs something like the old 'memo', which distils useful knowledge from the flood of data into a short high-frequency 'Flash Report' format. Also necessary is a strong chairman's office equipped with high-resolution sensors working with a VUCA-adapted 'scorecard' that accommodates and relates knowns, unknowns and unknowables.

Working sketch

A picture is emerging in this chapter of an organization that sees stability as an impossible dream in the VUCA world, and contrives to keep its balance by reconciling change and continuity, hope and fear, the vertical and horizontal dimensions, and the interests of the individual and the organization.

This recognition of the fragility of organizations in a VUCA world focuses the LFP company's attention on its organizational (Gemba) power. It sees its self-organizing Gemba Power as its essence: the muscles that provide its energy, the cellular structure that gives it eyes and ears, the locus of its thought and wisdom and the main generator of its reputations among its various constituencies.

The LFP company sets great store by its eyes and ears, and invests heavily in gathering and analyzing information. It is adapted to the age of 'big data' and prepared to act before all the evidence for the need to act is in.

This then is what an LFP organization *is*: inherently unstable, but operationally balanced, Gemba-centric (focused on the real, rather than the ideal), modular and self-organizing, data friendly.

The next chapter will focus on how such VUCA-adapted organizations can be guided, managed and improved.

---

[1] *Cultivating Gemba Power*: Toyo Keizai Inc., 2004.

[2] *In Data We Trust: How Customer Data Is Revolutionizing Our Economy*: Bloomsbury, 2012.

Chapter 8

Managing the LFP organization

At some point in the relatively recent past, developments that have been evident in the business environment for some years reached a critical point. The equivalent of a phase transition occurred and a new set of management challenges snapped into existence.

The globalization of marketplaces and supply chains, combined with instant communication through the global cloud, have multiplied the number of connections in all business networks and accelerated the speed at which effects follow causes, responses follow stimuli and consequences follow actions. Moreover, the links between cause and effect have become less clear: it is increasingly hard to work out what causes what, and the consequences that will follow from any given action.

It has been suggested in this book that the VUCA acronym summarizes the modern environment for business as well as for warfare.

But it's one thing to acknowledge the accelerating speed of change and its growing complexity, as well as the uncertainties, ambiguities and unpredictabilities they generate, and quite another to know how to handle or adapt to them.

The conventional management solution is to throw more resources at problems. If they are becoming more complex, then use the enormous power of modern computers to analyze the hell out of them. Or, as John Kotter has suggested, add a parallel system to your hierarchy to manage the complexity separately (see Chapter 3).

But this prescription is based on a misunderstanding of the nature of complexity and of 'complex' adaptive systems. Some problems are not merely extremely complicated, they're inherently complex, or, 'non-deterministic' as mathematicians say. They cannot be solved, or at any rate, there are no unique solutions to them. Complicated systems can be simplified. Complex systems can't be simplified: in such systems complexity is an inherent quality without which there would be no system.

It's not simply becoming more difficult to manage organizations in conventional ways, it's becoming virtually impossible.

So, in what ways, if not conventional ways, should organizations be managed in the VUCA world?

Even those not persuaded by Kotter's parallel, networked operating system solution will acknowledge his basic premise that some kind of blend of conventional and unconventional management is required for the time being, at any rate. But a hybrid system of this kind is not a solution. It is a patch on the conventional system, which should be seen as temporary or transitional. The Chinese operate a hybrid management system of which about 80% is home grown: the rest is the now dwindling legacy of imported ideas brought from the US by the 'sea-turtles' (see Chapter 4). It seems likely that, within a decade or two, only a few traces of the imported US system will survive in Chinese business.

Don't manage the unmanageable

The first step in addressing the new set of management problems is to acknowledge the existence of what one CEO called 'unmanageable complexity'. Learn to spot it, and then stand well clear. Attempts to manage unmanageable complexity almost always make things worse. Anthony Robbins, the self-help guru much quoted in the management literature, was wrong when he said, 'If you do what you've always done, you'll get what you've always gotten'. It doesn't work that way with complexity. If you do tomorrow what you did yesterday to a 'complex adaptive system', you are extremely unlikely to get the same result.

The second step when addressing the new management challenge is to acknowledge that the organizations best able to survive and thrive in an unmanageably complex environment are themselves unmanageably complex.

Complexity is nothing to be frightened of. It has always been part of our environment. Some find the patterns and pictures generated by complexity, such as the iconic Mandelbrot set, beautiful. It is certainly not something managers should attempt to eliminate. When your environment is complex, internal complexity is your friend.

In the VUCA world, complexity should be seen as an integral part of an organization's Gemba Power.

This book calls such internally complex VUCA-adapted organizations 'Light Footprint' (LFP) organizations. The VUCA world is invoking the LFP organization, just as it has invoked President Obama's LFP approach to warfare. LFP organizations aren't completely new. They are evolving from conventional organizations – in both the public and private sectors – just as the birds evolved from the dinosaurs and LFP warfare has evolved from Colin Powell's overwhelming force doctrine. The VUCA world is the LFP organization's environment of evolutionary adaptedness. Early manifestations of the LFP mutation include some aspects of the Apple management system, John Kotter's parallel operating system proposal and what the author has called 'China's Management Revolution'.[1]

Internally complex organizations aren't doomed to degenerate into hopeless chaos. Complex adaptive systems can be under control when no one is in control. They have self-organizing properties. One of the challenges facing managers in these volatile and complex times is to learn to trust people to manage themselves.

During the transition from being a conventional business to being an LFP organization, it may be wise to install parallel back-up systems similar to the Agile Combat Aircraft's triplex or quadruplex 'fly-by-wire' system (see Chapter 7).

The LFP organization organizes itself, within constraints. Some of these constraints, such as the culture, peer pressure, brands, and levels of fear, hope and trust are fuzzy and indistinct: they're 'emergent'. They can be nurtured or nudged to some extent, but not controlled. Others, such as inputs of people, money, technology or other resources can be controlled, although each exercise of such control is sure to have unintended consequences.

In short, today's business environment is unmanageably complex. To survive and thrive, organizations must be unmanageably complex too. Systems of this type, such as the LFP organization, can be influenced and guided by acting on border constraints and inputs.

As we have seen, the LFP-variant of the company differs in a number of important ways from the standard organization. It's more highly automated, for example; it's 'data friendly' and at home in cyber-space. It's modular. It's post-strategic. But it still needs to be managed in one way or another. Managers still need tools, models, techniques and methodologies to improve the profitability of their businesses and the efficiency of their organizations.

Of what kind should they be? Where can they be found?

LFP and conventional management

Management ideas are what Richard Dawkins calls 'memes' subject to natural selection (see Chapter 1). Their rise and fall reflect the changing business environment.

The advent of the VUCA world has changed the context of management so radically in recent years that the tools, ideas and approaches developed and refined over the decades to help managers manage are no longer fit for purpose.

It's probably the 'time compression', the increased speed at which events unfold, that has had the greatest impact. It became obvious during the 'dot.com' bubble at the end of the 1990s when it took only a few months for a newly listed company's market value to rival that of General Electric. The dramatic time compression of those years survived the bursting of the bubble in 2000 and has yet to ease. Consultancy assignments that once took six months now have be done in 12 weeks.

This time compression – combined with growing complexity, which meant that, however quickly they acted, managers could still not be sure the actions prescribed by conventional tools and techniques would have the predicted effects – cut a swathe through the world of management ideas. It was as if the planetoid VUCA had collided with our accumulated management wisdoms and caused a mass extinction.

But it is easy to be so overwhelmed by change that you forget what stays the same – and *how* it stays the same – can still enable organizations to change. The reverse is also true. As Tancredi says in Giuseppe di Lampedusa's famous 1958 novel, *Il Gattopardo* (The Leopard), 'Se vogliamo che tutto rimanga com'è bisogna che tutto cambi' ('If we want things to stay as they are, things will have to change').

In Charles Dickens's novel, *David Copperfield*, published in 1850 at the dawn of the modern corporate age, Wilkins Micawber tells the eponymous hero, 'Annual income twenty pounds, annual expenditure nineteen pounds nineteen and six, result happiness. Annual income twenty pounds, annual expenditure twenty pounds ought and six, result misery'. That's as true today as it ever was. Companies are still value-creating institutions. Cash is still their lifeblood. People are still their primary resource. Excessive costs are still their enemies. Risks need to be managed. Balance sheets need to be robust.

The context has changed, but the fundamentals remain the same. The new context requires some brand new tools, but it would be foolish to throw out a century of accumulated management wisdom and begin again from scratch. Just as mammals, birds and fish survived the great Cretaceous extinction, there are some management tools and ideas devised during the simpler, slower-paced business world of yesterday that, with some adaptation, will still be invaluable today.

Among these are what might be called 'purgative' models, developed to correct unforced errors and inefficiencies that, if unchecked, accumulate within an organization like sclerosis. They consist of processes, policies, practices that were rational and sensible at the time they were initiated, but which have since become redundant, or counter-productive. Purgative models are more important in the modern business world because the sclerotic accumulations they're designed flush out add weight and inertia to organizations and make them less agile.

Activity-based costing (ABC), as devised by Robert Kaplan and Thomas Johnson, and a technique developed by Mike Hammer and James Champy, known as business process re-engineering (BPR), are cases in point.

ABC says:

> Pay attention! The method you're using to assign costs to products and customers is out-dated. It may have been OK 70 years ago, but things have changed a lot since then and, if you look closely, you will find that you've been losing money on some customers and some products for a considerable time.

BPR says:

> Pay attention! Your business processes might have worked OK on the Ark, but a lot has changed since. New technologies offer enormous scope for increasing the efficiency of your processes. If you look closely, you will find many of your processes are superfluous, and most of the rest are extremely inefficient.

The kinship between these two ideas is clear. Both can trace their origins back to a common ancestor, the original purgative model, zero-based budgeting (ZBB), pioneered at Texas Instruments (TI) in the 1970s. This was a time of profound change in the young electronics industry, as integrated circuits began to replace transistors. It would be hard to prove, but it seems possible that TI's early use of ZBB had something to do with the fact that, having been an also-ran in transistors (it was the fifth largest producer in 1955), it had become the market leader in integrated circuits by 1975.

ZBB says:

> Pay attention! The ways you've been allocating resources are based on budgets set 10 years ago. A lot has changed since then. If you look closely, you will find some areas of the business are being starved of resources, while others are struggling to find uses for the resources they're allocated. You need to forget about the past and examine and justify each budget line individually.

All three of these health-check models have much to offer firms at a time such as the present when the pace of technological advance and the speed of change in the business environment are accelerating. The faster things change, the more quickly organizations drift out of fit with their environments and the more vigilant managers must be in policing 'unforced errors' such as out-dated cost accounting practices, inefficient or superfluous processes and inappropriate resource allocations.

But all three models share weaknesses: during a period of rapid and accelerating change, they are very expensive in terms of money and management resources, they take a long time and, as a result, there is a chance that in today's fast-changing VUCA environment, their prescriptions will be out-dated by the time the project has been completed.

Good management ideas can be adapted, however, just as life-forms adapt to their changing environments. ZBB, which is of great interest to organizations wishing to leave light footprints, because it deals with and aims to reduce organizational weight, is a case in point.

Rise and fall of ZBB

Government budgeting began in Great Britain after the enactment of the Bill of Rights in 1689, which transferred rights to levy taxes from the crown to the elected Parliament. By the early 19th century, the government was publishing detailed annual financial statements and projecting budget deficits or surpluses.

Although all US states were using annual budgets by the end of the 19th century, federal budgeting, despite several attempts, did not begin in earnest until the passage of the Budgeting and Accounting Act in 1921, which created a central Bureau of the Budget. It was not until the mid-1940s, however, that federal budgets described major goals and programs, analyzed supplies and needs and outlined long-range spending plans. In the 1960s, Lyndon Johnson's administration used the Planning–Programming–Budgeting System (PPBS) for the federal government. But the PPBS was abandoned in the 1970s by all federal departments apart from Defense.

Early business budgeting focused on controlling costs rather than measuring effectiveness. The use of budgets became more widespread in the private sector in the early 1900s because of the need for more careful planning in the era of mass production and budgeting began to be discussed in the management literature.

The problem with conventional 'rolling' or 'incremental' budgeting based on the previous year's budget – with variances derived, in an often unsystematic way, from the rate of inflation and the company's strategy – was that, in assuming next year would be much the same as the current year, it allowed the company's resource allocation to drift out of fit with the environment. Managers were not motivated to find less costly ways of operating and *were* motivated to avoid budget under-spends.

These widely-acknowledged weaknesses imposed adaptive pressures on the budgeting meme and prepared the way for the emergence of a new approach.

The key mutation came in a seminal article in the *Harvard Business Review* in 1970 by Peter Pyhrr, a manager at Texas Instruments (TI) in Dallas.[2] A book followed three years later.[3]

Pyhrr urged managers to ignore the previous year's budget when the time came to prepare the current year's. Rather, they should re-think everything from scratch. Take nothing for granted. Examine and justify every line. Treat all claims on resources equally, as if all of them were brand new. Is the line item necessary or could its objective be achieved in a less costly way, given modern technology?

It was a breath of fresh air; an antidote to the growing suspicion that, way below the threshold of the budgeting system's awareness, resource allocation errors were creeping in and the organization's overall efficiency was being gradually eroded by steady accretions of superfluous weight.

As articulated by Pyhrr, ZBB is related to the largely discredited PPBS. Both systems involve an evaluation of the inputs and outputs of activities, as opposed to the traditional line-item format. But ZBB had a much better name. In the constant struggle for survival in the meme world, labels and branding are vital. Lyndon Johnson's 'Planning–Programming–Budgeting System' wasn't the kind of moniker likely to stir the heart of even the nerdiest cost accountant. But 'zero-based budgeting' had something about it. It had presence in the meme world. It described itself perfectly and concisely and it cast the practitioner in the role of a Hercules purging the Augean stables of corporate inefficiency and waste.

An early convert was James (Jimmy) Carter, then governor of Georgia.

Impressed by Pyhrr's *HBR* article and subsequent book, Carter asked the TI man to apply his zero-based system to the state of Georgia budget in 1973. ZBB was not a success initially. The complexity of the state's finances made application of ZBB very costly in terms of both time and resources. But the meme adapted: it was refined and developed. By the time Governor Carter became President Carter in 1977 and introduced zero-based budgeting to Congress, the claim that ZBB had been a success at state level was plausible.

Carter's adoption of ZBB at federal level was a marketing coup and the system quickly 'gained traction', as modern parlance has it, in the private sector.

According to Richard Pascale's literature citations analysis,[4] ZBB had a decade of high visibility from the mid-1970s. By the end of the 1980s, citations were less frequent. Although still widely used by local and national governments and by health and education authorities, it had, until recently, largely fallen into disuse in the private sector. Its main weakness was that it was very time-consuming compared to traditional incremental budgeting, which has the great merit of simplicity. Although uncommon now as an annual exercise, ZBB survives, here and there, as a periodic health-check undertaken every three years or so. Another alleged problem with the system is that it's often undertaken for political reasons and is very susceptible to political influence.

But ZBB has left its mark. Even when it is not used, the fact that it could be used – that the ZBB procedures and processes are well-known and proven – imposes a discipline of a kind on the budgeting process. It has spawned derivatives such as activity-based costing (ABC) and business process re-engineering (BPR) that are still in use and it is one of those powerful general ideas that could make a comeback in the event of a change in the business context that favoured it or if it mutated in ways that addressed the weaknesses that led to its decline in popularity.

The second coming

These days, companies want to be lean, but not anorexic. They want to be low in fat, but not in muscle. They want to be fit for their purpose, which is to use what they are and what they could become to create value for their shareholders.

Lean means managers who do not waste money and time on inefficient procedures and superfluous or over-designed processes; managers at all levels who recognise, and try constantly to honour, their duty to shareholders to deliver to customers the best possible goods or services, as quickly as possible, at the lowest possible cost.

Lean means absence of waste, or *muda*, as they call it in Japan. In the Japanese lean canon there are seven wastes: excess inventory, excess production, excess processing, unnecessary movement, excess transport, wasted time and defects.

Companies want to be lean for two main reasons: first, because any superfluity in your operations consumes resources (free cash flow) that would otherwise have created value for shareholders; second, because excess fat is excess mass, which makes you less agile and less able to respond quickly to opportunities and threats.

Agile, nimble, light, quick on your feet: these are qualities that all companies aspire to in the modern business world characterized by accelerating change and growing complexity. This is zero-based budgeting territory par excellence. Purging an organization of all its accumulated *muda* is what ZBB and its derivatives is all about.

If ZBB didn't exist, someone would have to invent it.

But it does exist. Peter Pyhrr invented it four decades ago. It is part of the history of management ideas. Everyone who knows about ZBB knows it was tried, had some success, but was ultimately found wanting because its weaknesses proved greater than its strengths. So it was left there, on the shelf, gathering dust: an interesting experiment that had turned out to be a dead-end.

It took someone who knew very little about ZBB to revive it.

It sometimes happens that way. The history of scientific discovery is littered with stories of ignorant amateurs who wander up alleys the experts know are dead-ends and make breakthroughs. Ignorance of what is impossible sometimes makes it possible.

Two friends – the author and a former consultancy client – who had previously worked together, met for lunch at La Défense in Paris in June 2003. Both had moved on – one to a major oil company, the other to another consultancy. As friends do, they talked about this and that, where they were going and what they were doing. The oil company executive mentioned in passing that he had been working on an interesting ZBB project in the late 1980s. His friend knew next to nothing about ZBB. It had not been on Harvard Business School's curriculum when he was doing his MBA and it sounded dated. But he liked the idea conveyed by the name. Zero-base. *Tabula Rasa*. Start again from scratch. As luck would have it, he had a meeting with a banking client that afternoon to discuss a cost reduction project after a major post-merger integration they had done together.

He mentioned ZBB to the client but the client dismissed it out of hand.

'I know and like ZBB but we don't have the money for that, or the time. We need results in three months. ZBB takes a year, at least, just to do the base-line and the diagnostic.'

'Really?' thought the consultant. 'I didn't know that.'

But what he said was:

'Not necessarily.'

From ZBB to AZBB

Some old ideas are superfluous in the modern environment, some are inappropriate, some are counter-productive and some remain useful and can be adapted for use in the VUCA world.

So the question is: what attributes their original versions lacked would management interventions that are ostensibly useful in the VUCA world, such as ZBB, need to acquire, to survive and thrive in today's business environment?

The first is obvious. They must be faster: much faster.

Second, they have to be simple. The complicated cannot control the complex. Unmanageable complexity is bound to react in unexpected, and potentially disastrous, ways to attempts to interfere directly and in detail with its self-organizing processes – with its social interactions, its work relationships, unwritten rules, conventions and reflexes.

The third is less obvious, but related to the others: they must be 'bottom-up' projects, in which all those likely to be affected are involved in one way or another. This is partly because there is no time for the lengthy selling and implementation processes required in 'top-down' projects but mainly because in the modern world of unmanageable complexity, the outcomes from 'top-down' interventions tend to range from fruitless to disastrous.

Fast, simple, bottom-up: these are three essential qualities of an LFP-adapted intervention. Others include high precision, low-cost and, above all, light. Just as LFP companies tread lightly on the environments, so managers of LFP companies should tread lightly on their organizations.

The ZBB variant that emerged from the meeting in Paris in 2003 is called accelerated zero-based budgeting (AZBB) and the 'A' is not just a fourth letter (see box below).

LFP acronyms

A not entirely trivial characteristic of LFP-adapted interventions is that their adaptations are signified by the addition of a word to their names and thus a shift from three-letter to four-letter acronyms, as in the shift from ZBB to AZBB.

Other examples could include:

- From Value Based Management (VBM) to Integrated Value Based Management (IVBM), using wider definitions of 'value'.
- From Strategic Planning Process (SPP) to Adaptive Strategic Planning Process (ASPP), using estimates instead of budgets or plans.
- From Shareholder Value Model/Maximization (SVM) to Multiple Stakeholder Value Model (MSVM), as in Feng Jun's 'six wins' (see Chapter 4).
- From Competence Value Map (CVM) to Dynamic Competence Value Map (DCVM), looking at competence needs 10 years ahead.

- From Change Management Program (CMP) to Continuous Change Management Perspective/Program (CCMP), embedding a habit of constant, automatic adaptation in the organization's culture.

These transformations from three- to four-letter acronyms are meme analogues of gene mutations: the addition of a single DNA base to the DNA sequence that makes up the meme.

A suffix instead of a prefix can be added to indicate the area of application of very general principles such as LFP, e.g., LFPG (LFP Government); LFPA (LFP Administration); LFPW (LFP Welfare).

AZBB is like a drone: simple, cheap, minimal collateral damage and precisely targeted. As in *tai chi*, it uses its target module's own strengths to reform itself. It seems too good to be true: 15% cost savings delivered in 18 months at the most to the Profit and Loss Account, with service level agreements to which all are committed; no disruption of day-to-day business: all in 12 weeks. It's a glitch in the matrix – the first of a new generation of high-speed, targeted, light, high-intensity interventions that (like the new laser eye surgeries) blend diagnosis with treatment.

AZBB's speed is derived from three distinguishing characteristics.

1. Realistic

The ultimate aim of all interventions is to help your organization create more value with fewer resources. It has been estimated that a perfectly optimized activity would only require, on average, 50–60% of the resources used pre-optimization. But not all of these potential savings are accessible. Many lie hidden in the nooks and crannies of business units, functions and departments or are held in reserve for contingencies, such as a sudden deterioration in the business environment or an unexpected request from the CEO. Many are too deeply-embedded, too subtle or require too much time, analysis, effort and disruption for their extraction to be worthwhile. And in a VUCA world time, is of the essence. By the time you have identified and analysed every last bit of waste or redundancy, it may be too late. AZBB doesn't engage in large Business Process Re-engineering (BPR), or other projects that require substantial investments of time and money. It focuses exclusively on what can be accomplished within 18 months.

And even if all these reserves and redundancies were accessible, it would not be wise to attempt to eliminate them altogether. The LFP company needs some redundancy. An organization screwed down tight as a nut, with not an ounce of fat or superfluity, is like a robot. It lacks the creativity, innovative energy and agility it needs to thrive in a VUCA world. Previously, becoming ultra-lean was sometimes a winning play. It won't be like that again.

AZBB doesn't try to optimise. It aims to improve significantly and to leave the module better equipped to improve itself further. As one CEO who had used AZBB put it, 'It's like mowing a lawn, simple and effective, but it must be done regularly to keep the lawn neat and tidy.'

2. Focus on decision units

ZBB focuses on the 'decision package' (see below) while AZBB focuses on the people, the 'decision unit'.

Standard Zero-Based Budgeting

Standard zero-based budgeting (ZBB) requires managers to develop a 'decision package' (DP) for each project or activity. DPs normally include descriptions of purpose, analyses of costs and opportunity costs (next best courses of action), performance metrics, benefits and the consequences of abandoning the activity.

Each proposed dollar of spending must be accompanied by a detailed account of what it will be spent on including purchases and labour hours required, a description of potential problems, and estimates of the costs of resolving them.

In addition to identifying and analyzing the costs and benefits of other methods of performing each activity, each DP also identifies different levels of performance for each option. This is normally done by establishing a minimum spending level (75% of the current level, say) and developing separate DPs that include the costs and benefits of additional levels of spending for that activity. This analysis allows managers to consider a lower than current level of spending or even the abandonment of the activity.

Once developed, the DPs for both old and new projects are ranked in order of importance to allow managers to identify priorities and the leadership to evaluate and compare the needs of individual units or divisions when allocating resources.

The main problem with standard ZBB is that it consumes substantial amounts of management time and you cannot be sure beforehand that the benefits of the ZBB exercise will exceed the opportunity costs so incurred. There are also costs associated with the risks that problems and frictions may arise during the implementation phase of what is essentially a top-down intervention.

A compromise that eases, but doesn't solve, the problem is to blend incremental rolling budgets with ZBB: to retain the latter for the annual budgets, for example, and perform a ZBB exercise every four years, say, or when a major change occurs, such as a merger.

An AZBB exercise begins with the identification of target Decision Units (DUs) – usually no more than 50 people under a manager – and non-negotiable savings objectives to which the DU manager commits. These are the modules of an LFP organization. The ground rules are spelled out: no taboos (nothing is undiscussed, or undiscussable); detailed monitoring throughout the project; continuous validation of proposals and trade-offs; the DU manager, working with a few of his, or her colleagues, takes the lead and presents the results to the board.

The AZBB process takes 12 weeks in all and is usually divided into three four-week phases:

Phase 1 – ABC, identify mission, activities and costs.

Phase 2 – identify levers, service levels and improvement options.

Phase 3 – align savings with budgets, link to processes and organizational charts.

The AZBB process begins with an activity-based costing (ABC) phase based on existing budgets, designed to elicit a good understanding of the DU's missions, activities and costs. This is the AZBB drone in reconnaissance mode. It takes four weeks and is followed by an iterative, 'bottom-up' participative phase to identify improvement options, such as re-defining missions, activities and service levels and how to effect them, by resource pooling, for instance, or process and interface improvements. This also takes four weeks. It can produce proposals to increase, as well as decrease, budgets for particular activities. A final four-week phase aligns savings with the overall budget and links them into control processes and functional charts.

In this age of 'lean', it is usually assumed that all areas of the business are over-spending and/or over-staffed to some extent. No such assumptions are made in an AZBB project. It is accepted that AZBB may reveal that some functions (compliance, risk management, marketing, for instance) or activities are genuinely under-staffed and lack the resources to carry out the missions assigned to them.

During Phases 2 and 3, therefore, DU managers working with finance and HR can present for validation by management or the board 'Re-Investment Areas', where additional people and other resources are required.

3. Cross-functional

AZBB involves from the outset two key enabling functions – finance and human resources (HR) – that are either forgotten, or called on too late in conventional efficiency improvement projects.

Finance is vital because it's the only department that can confirm the cost baseline, validate savings calculations and monitor their delivery. Working together, the finance department and DU manager incorporate the improvement plans and levers in a revised budget – it is not called AZB Budgeting for nothing – to which both parties are jointly committed.

The HR department is often called in at the end of a traditional cost reduction project, and asked to help with implementation. No heed is paid to their ritual complaint that the plan won't work because the human element and the feasibility of changing the organization and removing or moving people were not taken into account.

In AZBB, the HR department are involved even before the start. They plan the journey with the DU manager and validate its feasibility in HR terms. When the project begins, they usually observe in Phase 1, participate in Phase 2 and work closely on implementation plans in Phase 3.

They help the DU manager draft the detailed action plan and design the personnel deployments and re-deployments required to achieve everything in 18 months. New organization charts are developed for each phase and may go through four editions during the 18 months.

HR plays a crucial role in LFP organizations, because, as with the Agile Combat Aircraft (see Chapter 7), the main constraints on the agility of organizations are the 'wetware' (human beings).

Enlightening

In a complex VUCA world, with its daily data overloads and frequent changes of position and orientation, leaders and managers may find it hard to keep tabs on what they're managing. The three-step AZBB process helps them to get to know their organization, its mission, its activities and its people far better then they would ever have thought possible in 12 weeks. As already noted, the leaders of LFP organizations must steer well clear of day-to-day management, but they need to develop an intimate understanding of the organization and of the strengths and limitations of its Gemba Power.

During the height of the 'empowerment' fad in the 1990s, there was much talk of 'de-layering' and 'horizontal management'. The idea was that organizations were easier to manage with fewer management levels. The law of unintended consequences intervened: it soon became clear that the opposite was the case. When a manager's span of control is too wide, he or she cannot know everyone, let alone what everyone is doing.

In retrospect, the de-layering 'fad' seems like a futile attempt to simplify the complex. There's plenty of hierarchy, both within and between the modules of the LFP organization, but it is 'emergent' rather than mandated. It's constantly re-configuring itself and is maintained by trust rather than power or authority.

Without hierarchy and the filtering and delegation associated with it, it would be impossible to manage large organizations in a VUCA world.

AZBB projects enlighten the organization itself as well as its top managers.

Despite the fact that it is an accelerated intervention and is not officially looking at the organization, a common by-product of an AZBB project is more efficient organization both within and across the DUs. The AZBB process leads to a deeper understanding of the organization's costs and key cost drivers. Because the project is both bottom-up and comprehensive, it generates the information needed to build accurate cost models that can be used subsequently to re-calibrate budgets as cost drivers evolve. Another benefit is that, once built and agreed, these cost models improve the quality of budget discussions between finance people, DU managers and the board or executive committee.

During the project, the DU looks at itself and at all the external and internal clients and suppliers that depend on it and upon which it depends. This horizontal, value-chain, perspective often reveals opportunities for simplifications, reorganizations and mergers of DUs. Because these rationalization opportunities are revealed by a local bottom-up, DU-led exercise and not demanded by a grand top-down strategy that the DU has played no part in developing, they're relatively easy to implement within the 18 month AZBB window.

Restructurings, including fissions, fusions and closures, inspired by an AZBB exercise, are seldom controversial because they emerge from a process in which everyone is involved and serve an ethos of self-improvement to which everyone is committed.

Cohesion

An AZBB exercise also helps to improve the cohesion of modular LFP organizations by requiring conversations between several different functions and management levels.

In conventional organizations, conversations between the top level of management (N) and the third level of management (N-2) – where most DU managers are to be found – are rare because it is usually seen as 'politically incorrect' for N to talk to N-2 alone without N-1 being actively involved.

AZBB is unusual in being a project initiated by N, but directed at N-2. This provides a rare opportunity for N, N-1 and N-2 to build or reinforce their trust in one another. The AZBB system motivates N-2 Decision Unit managers to be candid about their costs and thus gives N a unique insight into redundancies hidden away in DU nooks and crannies to cover contingencies.

N, N-1 and N-2 all attend the final AZBB discussions and together validate the mission, the activities and resources required to enable the DU to perform well. They agree on matters N will never ask about again and on the level of service that N-1 and N-2 will provide to N. Without intending to, at this meeting they effectively sign the most important agreement in an LFP organization: one that sets out the relationship between the modules (DUs) and the centre. It is a trust-building meeting. Everyone realizes how much more efficient the organization can be when they talk the same language, know each other's expectations and understand what can really be delivered, by when.

Trust is everything in an LFP organization because without it, the centre cannot 'empower' modules to organize and manage themselves.

There was much talk of 'empowerment' and, by implication, trust in the 1990s. In her book, *When Giants Learn to Dance,* Harvard Business School professor, Rosabeth Moss Kanter, said that companies were most productive when employees were empowered to make decisions on their own: she urged companies to dismantle their hierarchies, and allow employees to 'dance'.[5]

A decade later, another HBS professor, Chris Argyris, said that the empowerment experiment had been a failure.[6]

Argyris argued that the purpose of 'empowerment' is to improve the company's performance by achieving the 'internal', as opposed to the 'external', commitment of employees. Only external commitment, where employees merely comply with the terms of their contracts, is possible when the tasks and the behaviour required to perform them are set by others and performance goals and priorities are set by management. Internal commitment becomes possible only if employees are empowered to define their own tasks, and how to achieve them, and if goals and priorities are set jointly by employees and management.

The experiment failed, according to Argyris, because although CEOs paid lip-service to the then fashionable idea of empowerment, ultimately they were unwilling to surrender enough of their power to achieve 'internal' commitment.

There's no place for 'control freaks' in LFP organizations, or for those who relish the benefits of empowerment but are unwilling to accept the responsibilities or accountabilities that come with it. Trust is a two-way street. It is not easy for leaders to give but they should remember that it is the foundation stone of corporate governance. Whenever investors buy shares in companies, they place their trust in the managers, as their agents, to spend their money wisely and not to impose excessive 'agency costs'.

AZBB builds trust, because its prescriptions emerge from bottom-up processes and, because, quite incidentally, it provides a space in which people at all levels, in all functions (N, N-1, N-2, finance and HR, for example), can make personal, face-to-face declarations of mutual trust.

A tool for VUCA times

AZBB seems at first sight to be a modest, tactical intervention. A quick, rough-and-ready fix that's hardly worth bothering with when much more could be achieved by a major, organization-wide intervention that leaves no stone unturned and no improvement lever un-pressed.

An AZBB project is just mowing the lawn when the whole garden could be landscaped.

But this modesty of ambition is deceptive.

AZBB delivers what it's supposed to, i.e., a 15% cost savings in 18 months from a 12-week project with no disruptions of day-to-day business. AZBB projects focused on a total cost base of over $10bn all over the world have delivered average cost savings of over 15% for all kinds of DUs (including commercial, marketing, logistics and support functions) all realized in the P&L within 18 months, fully accepted by DU managers, validated by the Finance Departments and all with the active involvement of Human Resources Departments.

But AZBB does much more than that too.

Its power comes not so much from what it does at the time, as from what it leaves behind: accurate cost models, relevant and up-to-date reporting systems, agreed service levels, mutual understandings and trust at all levels, across every plane.

AZBB is quick, but not superficial; the work is done by the DUs themselves and the results emerge from a 'bottom-up' process. It is self-improvement, rather than imposed improvement. Frictions tend to be minimal because, in LFP organizations, the modules want to be more efficient.

An LFP organization is a set of self-managed, self-improving, data friendly 'modules', patrolled by remotely controlled 'intervention drones', such as AZBB. Most of the lawn-mowing is done by the DUs or modules themselves, with some help from well-trained and well-informed 'special forces' teams. Constant improvement is routine: just one aspect of the constant change that true LFP organizations become accustomed to.

Senior managers of an LFP organization recognize that the focus of their attention should be on the borders and constraints of their self-managing modules. They set targets, but they won't always say how those targets should be approached or achieved.

When deployed in a conventional organization, AZBB delivers what it promises: that is often enough. But for an organization whose leaders wish to adapt better to the VUCA world, AZBB's bottom-up, DU-focused, inclusive, consensual and trust-building qualities could also leave behind prepared ground, seeded with LFP potential (see Chapter 10).

---

[1] *China's Management Revolution: Spirit, Land, Energy*: Palgrave Macmillan, 2011.

[2] 'Zero-Base Budgeting': *Harvard Business Review*, Nov./Dec. 1970.

[3] *Zero-Base Budgeting: A Practical Management Tool for Evaluating Expenses*: John Wiley, 1973.

[4] *Managing on the Edge: How Successful Companies Use Conflict to Stay Ahead*: Simon & Schuster, 1990.

[5] *When Giants Learn to Dance: Mastering the Challenge of Strategy, Management and Careers in the 1990s*: Simon & Schuster, 1989.

[6] 'Empowerment: The Emperor's New Clothes': *Harvard Business Review*, May–June 1998.

Chapter 9

Enlightened leadership

Throughout what Walter Kiechel calls 'The Management Century', from the publication in 1911 of Frederick Taylor's book *Principles of Scientific Management* to the present day, two views of the company have vied with each other for ascendancy: the company as a machine and the company as a community of people.[1]

Taylor's 'machine' view dominated initially, but the beginnings of a community view began to emerge in the inter-war years from Elton Mayo's Hawthorne experiments (1924–32). Workers were not automata, Mayo showed: they have feelings and how they feel affects how much they produce.

From this idea that people are 'soft cogs' in the machine and must be treated well if the machine is to work properly, emerged Peter Drucker's concept of the company as a social institution. Douglas McGregor further elevated the role of humans in the machine, when he suggested in 1960 that people were not naturally lazy and in need of policing (theory X). According to McGregor, people hungered not for an easy work life, but for meaning in their work, and would contribute positively if their work was well-designed (theory Y).

The subsequent rise of an active, as opposed to adaptive, approach to management, also associated with Peter Drucker, led to a switch of focus back to the machine view. This was exemplified by the new 'strategic' approach to management, pioneered by Bruce Henderson's Boston Consulting Group, with its 'experience curve' and 'growth share matrix' (see Chapter 1). The machine became more aggressive and acquisitive: too aggressive for some, as the popularity of J. K. Galbraith's 1967 book, *The New Industrial State*, showed. The book marked something of a watershed in the public view of business. In a 1966 Harris poll, 55% of respondents said they had 'a great deal of confidence' in the leaders of large companies. Nine years later the figure was down to 15%.

The machine view remained in the ascendant throughout the Japanese invasion of western markets in the 1970s and 1980s. The corporate control market remained active, Michael Porter's 'strategy' ideas and frameworks gained currency and finance professors moved up the business school pecking order.

Since then, the company as a machine and the company as a community views have lived together like two ill-assorted siblings under the parental control of the high-profile 'leader'.

The origins of the idea that great leaders can, with their mastery of the science and art of management, concentrate and focus all of an organization's resources – human, technical and financial – and win in the marketplace against all the odds, can be traced back to Lee Iacocca's appointment as CEO of Chrysler in 1978.

Chrysler was on the brink of collapse when Iacocca, recently fired by Ford (where he had been president) after falling out with Henry Ford II, arrived. Within three years, Chrysler was back in profit and continued to flourish under his leadership until he retired in 1992.

So great was his fame by then that his book, *Iacocca: An Autobiography*, co-written with William Novak (Bantam, 1984) was the best-selling non-fiction hardback book in both 1984 and 1985. *Talking Straight*, (Bantam, 1988), a response to Sony founder Akio Morita's book, *Made in Japan* (Dutton, 1986), praising American creativity, was likewise a big seller.

Although it has had some setbacks in recent years, particularly in the banking sector, the idea of the all-powerful, all-knowing and omnicompetent company leader is still the conventional wisdom and has reconciled, after a fashion, the tension between the machine and community views of the company. Leaders become leaders, according to the leader-centric view of management, because they can run the machine *and* the community: they can manage the hard *and* the soft; the numbers *and* the stories; the money *and* the people; the hearts *and* the minds.

It seems fair to say that most of the leaders in the current epoch of leadership have, with some exceptions, been more concerned with the machine than the community. But thanks partly to wider social pressures, the community has done OK too. As Kiechel pointed out in the *HBR*, 'people expect to be treated with fairness and respect even if long-term job security is less assured. Blatant sexism, naked bullying and outrageous managerial behaviour are more likely to be called out'.

But it also seems fair to say that consensus has yet to be reached on what makes a good company leader. Perhaps the answer depends to some extent on when and in what environment the question is asked. Kiechel suggests: 'Recovering or reimagining authentic, satisfying sources of executive authority, will be high on the to-do list for management's next century. '

LFP leadership

Since management's next century will unfold in the VUCA world and, since it has been suggested in this book that what has been called the LFP organization is best-equipped to thrive in a VUCA environment, it is worth speculating a little about what sort of qualities might be expected in a successful LFP leader.

1. Being leader

The shift in focus from the company as a machine to the company as a community is a shift of focus from what the company *does* to what the company *is*: from action to essence.

As with a conventional company, an LFP company is both machine and community. But it's an unconventional kind of machine in which the agency is distributed among self-managing modules instead of being concentrated in the CEO. And it is also an unconventional business community: its modular structure makes it more like a federation or group of communities with a shared sense of fate, than a single coherent corporate society.

There are some decisions that lead to action or inaction that only the leader can make in an LFP organization – give the go ahead, or say 'stop'; reject or select this design or that course of action; break ties in arguments and debates; hire her; fire him; allocate federal (as opposed to module) resources. But relatively few decisions pass all the subsidiarity gates and land on the leader's desk. Those that do end up there because it is the leader's job to make such decisions, not because of the leader's qualities as a manager or a person.

A much more important leadership role in the LFP organization than taking decisions is *being* the organization; cultivating, nurturing and articulating that shared sense of fate and overall vision that holds the modules together. This is the role of the 'strategus'.

2. Leaders and emotions

When the company as machine was the dominant view, a dispassionate and calculating leader was favoured; someone who could keep his or her eye on the fundamentals – the share price, or free cash flow – and wouldn't be distracted by misplaced sentiment or the idea that the company had obligations to non-owning constituencies.

In a VUCA world where a minor rudeness or a careless disregard for people's feelings and sensitivities can be reported to the cloud, and precipitate a serious crisis out of a chance remark the leader might have forgotten almost immediately, a dispassionate leader is a liability.

The LFP organization is adapted to the storm of emotion constantly blowing through the VUCA world. Its substance, the shared sense of destiny and the common vision that unite the modules and give them a sense of direction is pure emotion. In the LFP organization, the human component (the 'wetware') is fully accepted as a constraint and a source of strength. Without emotion, the modules would not cling together and act in concert. They are like cells – each has its own nucleus, but all carry the same emotional genes. It is the leader's job to write and refine the code on the genes, and ensure its high-fidelity replication when it's time for mitosis.

The leader cares for the emotional environment: the ambience, the ethos, the history and traditions, those unique moments that unite people (achieving the impossible, or averting a great danger), the smell of the place.

Steve Jobs invested a lot of time and passion in the design of the Pixar headquarters at Emeryville. He 'obsessed over every aspect of the new building from the overall concept to the tiniest detail regarding materials and construction', Walter Isaacson reported in his biography.[2] The overall concept was an open space round a central atrium, designed to encourage random encounters. 'There's a temptation, in our networked age to think that ideas can be developed by email and iChat,' said Jobs. 'That's crazy. Creativity comes from spontaneous meetings, from random discussions. You run into someone, you ask what they are doing, you say "Wow," and soon you're cooking up all sorts of ideas.'

3. Leaders and followers

In the LFP organization, leaders and followers are symbionts – the matched pair of leader and army in the Greek idea of 'strategus'. The one both shapes and reflects the other. In an organization in which agency (the right to act) is distributed among the modules, there is no need for a man or woman of action at the top. The guru or artist leader is preferable; the keeper of the knowledge, and ethos; the wise rather than the strong; Ghandi or Mandela rather than Alexander or Napoleon.

Some Chinese leaders are like this: Feng Jun and his 'six wins' or Jack Ma teaching his executives *tai chi*, *Jinyu* ('keeping silent') and *jingzuo* ('meditation') and believing that the hardest tasks for an entrepreneur are to 'rise above the self' and keep a habit of introspection while adapting to the changing world (see Chapter 4).

The very word 'leader', as in someone 'in the lead' or 'ahead', can be *mis*leading in an LFP organization. In the paradoxical LFP world, a remark attributed to the 19th century French politician Alexandre Ledru-Rollin has a curious resonance: 'There go the people. I must follow them, for I am their leader.'

4. Consistency

Leaders lead in several settings: in the office, where colleagues are colleagues; in private where colleagues are friends; in small, intimate groups; and in more formal settings, with large audiences at conferences, or presentations to employees, investment analysts or the financial press.

In the LFP company, leaders must operate consistently in all these settings. If they pose and posture, and assume different personae in different settings, their authenticity could be questioned and others may find it hard to trust them.

Walter Isaacson's fine biography of the late Steve Jobs leaves the reader in no doubt that Jobs was prickly and occasionally bullying and ill-mannered. Even so, he was respected and cherished by Apple people, who shed more than a few tears when he died on October 5, 2011. Jobs's chosen successor, Tim Cook, Apple's long-time head of operations, is a very different personality. Jobs knew that when he appointed Cook his heir apparent. In an interview at the end of 2012, Cook recalled that Jobs had said to him, 'I never want you to ask what I would have done. Just do what's right'.[3]

All sorts of personality types can work as LFP company leaders, as long as they are consistent and as long as the people are content with the way their leader represents them.

Chinese entrepreneur, Yuan Yafei, founder of HTSB group, which has interests in retailing, manufacturing, finance and real estate, told the author, 'I'm a dictator'. Yuan believes that to create a family spirit in his business he has to 'control the minds' of his 15,000 employees. He grew up in a military family and manages his group like an army.[4]

And appearances can be deceptive.

At first sight, chefs seem to be bad role models for leaders. 'When you walk into a kitchen,' said Michael Brimm, Emeritus Professor of Organization and Management at INSEAD, the environment 'appears to violate practically every modern management precept. The chef is a dictator, barking out orders and maintaining a rigid discipline. There's very little participation. And talk of "empowerment" would be greeted with howls of derisive laughter by the staff.'

But ask staff why they work for a pittance, in terrible conditions under tyrannical leaders, and many will say they would pay to work with such chefs because they're learning so much. Brimm asked one apprentice chef whose dish had been binned by the chef because it was too salty, 'doesn't it ever get to you that you never get any praise?'. The apprentice looked at him in astonishment. 'But I do! Didn't you see those times when chef walked by, tasted, and walked on, without saying anything? That was great praise. He was telling me that I had got it right.'

5. Plural leadership

In the voluminous literature on company leadership, it's frequently said that leadership is not confined to the C-suite, that there is leadership at all levels of the hierarchy.

In conventional organizations run by hard-driving CEOs, it's often hard to see this distributed leadership at work. In a modular, LFP organization it's obvious. Each module has to be led in one way or another, although not necessarily by the same person, all the time and in every situation.

In the LFP company, leadership is both centralized and personified, and de-centralized and distributed. Each employee will feel, from time to time, that 'the leader here is me', or 'the leader is us'. When you act and think as one, it's often hard to say who's in the lead.

Remember that Lao Tzu saying in Chapter 6: 'When the best leader's work is done the people say, "We did it ourselves".'

6. Leaders and trust

Leaders of LFP companies take pains to earn a reputation for being trustworthy, and are predisposed to see strangers (both corporate and individual) as potential friends rather than enemies. They may seem naïvely trusting, but there is nothing naïve about it. It is simply a recognition that in the VUCA world companies need friends and the best way to forge new friendships is to trust people until they prove untrustworthy.

As we saw in Chapter 7, the LFP company plays 'tit-for-tat' in its business relationships. It trusts initially, retaliates right away if its trust is betrayed, forgives if a betrayer repents and plays the same way all the time, so that everyone knows what to expect.

LFP leaders play tit-for-tat themselves, and embed the approach in the modules so that it becomes an integral part of the brand.

This predisposition to trust opens up space for new collaborations and partnerships and, by dispensing with lengthy negotiations over detailed contracts and partnership agreements, greatly accelerates the process of relationship-building.

7. Leadership and speed

Because they know that in a VUCA world a decision delayed is often an opportunity lost, leaders of LFP organizations pride themselves on their reaction times. In decision-making, the sooner is almost always the better. The losses incurred when it is not are unlikely to be significant compared to the benefits of speed.

The speed comes not from hastiness, but from a well-equipped group of analysts and advisers dedicated to serving the leader. This is the leader's module or *dong ban*, as the Chinese call it. Decisions can be made quickly, because the leader's staff provide the information needed to make well-informed decisions quickly.

The well-staffed leader's office violates the conventional symbol of lean organization; namely the lean head office. LFP organizations don't favour the remote leader, making decisions on his or her own. They know that in a VUCA world issues are too complex for individuals, however able or knowledgeable, to make important decisions without support and advice. Speed is vital, but so is consensus. Leaders who make decisions 'off-the-cuff', without consulting, will not be trusted or followed.

Leaders for all seasons

In conventional companies there's a tendency, these days, for CEOs to see themselves as just passing through; as being on a stepping-stone to greater things. They're like football stars signed for a year or two with a minor league club, with their sights set firmly on the Premier League. 'Do well here, and you will be spotted by a scout (head-hunter) from a big club,' they tell themselves.

The fates of the leader and the company are not aligned, let alone shared.

LFP company leaders are there for the duration. They're integrated with the organization. The feel close to it and its people. They understand their company and cannot imagine doing better anywhere else. Most people interested in business would have been amazed if Steve Jobs had suddenly announced, a few years after his return to Apple, that he was leaving to be CEO of Hewlett Packard or Sony.

They also understand their company's position in the VUCA business environment.

Leaders of conventional companies are sitting in the driver's seat, gripping the steering wheel. When it's hot, they reach for the air-con; when it's cold, they turn on the heater; when its getting dark, they turn on the lights; when it starts to rain, they turn on the windscreen wipers. They keep their eyes on the road and follow the satnav's instructions. They and the company are insulated from the outside a world; a capsule travelling through time on paved roads towards a pre-determined destination.

LFP company leaders are walking through the countryside, gazing at the view, stopping from time to time to look at a flower, leaving the path to examine a ruin, listening to birds, insects, and a dog fox barking in the distance. They have a destination, but the walk itself is the real objective. Their route meanders, depending on the topography and interesting features they might see in the middle distance. They're not simply passing through. They are part of the countryside. They feel it, see it, smell it.

Another characteristic of leaders of LFP companies is that they're pragmatists. In the VUCA world, idealism will lead you astray. VUCA requires people who look at the world as it is, not as they would like it to be, and who take one step at a time in what seems to be roughly the right direction.

The vital importance of pragmatism in the VUCA world is evident in recent developments in philosophy.

From ideal to real

There are two ways to approach the problem of injustice. The first is to identify the institutions that characterize a perfectly just society and seek to establish them. This was the approach adopted by Thomas Hobbes, John Locke, Jean-Jacques Rousseau, Immanuel Kant and, more recently, the late John Rawls. Amartya Sen has called it 'transcendent institutionalism'. It sees justice as emerging from just institutions such as parliamentary democracy, secret ballots, the separation of judicial, legislative and executive powers, free speech and equality before the law. Taken together, these institutions represent an ideal, to which all societies should aspire.[5]

Insofar as any are absent, defective, or ineffective there will be injustice.

The focus of this standard, contractarian theory of justice is the ideal. Much attention is paid to its foundations, the intricacy of the inter-relations of its elements, the details of its structure, its adaptation to the evolving socio-economy, and its engagement with other, less just creeds and societies. It considers only the imperfections of actual societies, the areas where and the extents to which they're less than ideal – their institutional deficiencies in other words.

The other approach is to focus on actual societies and to identify and seek to address the most obvious injustices.

Sen calls this approach 'realization-focused comparison' and cites equally illustrious antecedents. It was the approach of Adam Smith (in *The Theory of Moral Sentiments*), Nicolas de Condorcet, Jeremy Bentham, Mary Wollstonecraft, Karl Marx, John Stuart Mill and, much earlier, of Confucius (see box below).

Confucius and the European Enlightenment

Confucian thought was brought to Europe by Jesuits who had lived in China during the European Enlightenment. Gottfried Leibniz, for example, saw similarities between his and Confucian philosophy. Leibniz's ideas of 'simple substance' and 'pre-established harmony' are said to have been influenced by similar, much older, Confucian ideas.

The French philosopher Voltaire saw, in Confucian rationalism, the perfect foil for Christian dogma. He praised Confucian ethics and politics, and suggested China's socio-political structure could be a model for Europe.

'Confucius has no interest in falsehood,' Voltaire said. 'He did not pretend to be a prophet; he claimed no inspiration; he taught no new religion; he used no delusions; flattered not the emperor under whom he lived.'

Much has been written about the strong correspondences between the Confucian philosophy and the ideas of Adam Smith, expressed in the *Theory of Moral Sentiments*. Both were empirical, in that they were based on observations of human nature, rather than deduced from a set of first principles. And both concluded that the propensity to behave in a moral way was an integral part of human nature.

Real societies, according to these thinkers, are what we have and, notwithstanding their institutional weaknesses and departures from the ideal, we must try to make them more just.

There are overlaps between the two approaches. What constitutes an obvious injustice in an actual society will be decided, to a large extent, by reference to an idea of justice similar to the ideal in 'transcendent institutionalism' (TI). And efforts to correct or to address manifest injustice in actual societies will often take the form of attempts to establish just institutions.

The difference lies in emphasis and focus. The first approach is inherently idealistic, the second is inherently pragmatic.

Equivalents of the idealistic TI approach abound in the management literature. Although, thanks to the Internet, markets are becoming more efficient (see Chapter 7), The Efficient Market Hypothesis is widely acknowledged to be unrealistic. It is regarded as a useful fiction, however, and retains a strong hold on the imaginations of financial economists.

The idea that efficient markets value firms by capitalizing their prospective free cash flows remains an important consideration for company leaders, particularly those with significant equity-linked incentive packages.

The idea of the strategy-led company, in the conventional sense of a 'strategy' as a plan, is classically idealistic. It is not as dominant in practice as it is usually assumed to be (putatively 'brilliant strategies' are often *ex post* descriptions of sequences of actions that were essentially tactical when they were taken, to which strategic logic is imputed retrospectively), but the notion that a company today is the realization of the strategic intent of its leadership yesterday, is more or less taken for granted.

The plan, or 'strategy', is derived from a detailed analysis of the company's initial position on its 'value chain' consisting of its customers, suppliers and competitors, its competitive advantages and disadvantages, expectations about how things will change over the planning period and steps that will need to be taken to reach the targets in the CEO's Long Term Incentive Plan by the due dates. The context for planning is provided by a conceptual framework, such as Michael Porter's 'five forces'.

Porter's 'five forces' are still a useful guide for data gathering and his 'value chain' was an illuminating concept, but the generic strategies derived from them are hopelessly idealistic. As Gary Hamel ('Strategic intent and core competences', see Chapter 1) put it, 'Porter's model is to business success what Biblical exegesis is to sainthood. You can study it all you want, but you will never get there'.

The strategy, or plan, plays the same role in business as the ideal plays in Sen's TI (transcendent institutionalism) approach to the problem of injustice. It imagines the ideal alignment of a company with its environment and focuses exclusively on achieving such an alignment. It pays very little attention to the practical problems associated with inevitable mis-alignments.

Corporate purpose

The most powerful idea in conventional, 'idealistic', management is that a company is nothing more than a mechanism for creating value for its shareholders. Its power lies in the fact that it is true. A company has no purpose other than shareholder value maximization (SVM), although it is not so much a purpose as a *raison d'être*, or a fate bequeathed to it by the logic of the capitalist system.

Capital moves to its highest value use. If a company declared that (or behaved as if) it regarded SVM as subordinate to some higher purpose, such as supplying quality goods and services to customers or quality of life to employees or other 'stakeholders', it would become less attractive to investors, which would cause its cost of capital to rise and its ability to achieve any purpose to fall.

A more sophisticated version of the idea is that the popularity of the 'stakeholder' model – that shareholders are one of a number of constituencies with legitimate claims on the value a firm creates – stems from the mistaken belief that SVM is irreconcilable with 'higher' aims, such as serving customers, caring for employees and the environment or being a responsible corporate citizen.

Companies are not free to choose their purposes, but they are both free and duty bound to choose ways to maximize shareholder value.

Although only shareholders can hold companies *to account*, companies that fail to take *into account* the interests of other groups, such as employees, customers, suppliers and local communities, may find it hard to create value for anyone.

Because SVM is hardly a goal that can stir the blood and inspire extraordinary effort, other purposes, visions or missions may need to be invoked. But it is wrong, according to this view, to see a vision as having priority over, or as being in some sense 'higher', than the goal of SVM. Visions and missions are 'marketing': merely means of achieving the end of creating value for shareholders, not ends in themselves.

But that does not mean appealing to the SVM company's non-existent better nature is pointless. Such appeals are messages from outside about the value of the various classes of reputational asset and so convey information to SVM firms. And volunteering, philanthropy and Corporate Social Responsibility (CSR) projects involve the SVM company's employees who do have 'better natures'.

To minimize the cost of financial capital, firms must appear to be 'value hunters': but to minimize the cost of human capital (and to attract and keep employees and customers), firms must also appear to be 'value givers'.

This is where the debate gets interesting for the VUCA-adapted LFP company. Questions of purpose and the creation and distribution of shareholder value are largely irrelevant in a volatile, uncertain world where nothing is quite what it seems and each action is sure to have unintended consequences. The quality above all that LFP companies need to thrive in a VUCA world is the ability to attract and keep good people.

Corporate pragmatism

Like Sen's 'realization-focused comparison' (RC) philosophers, LFP firms are pragmatists, not idealists. Each has a strong sense of who it is, and what it can do, and a misty and constantly changing vision of the future and of the opportunities it might offer. It's alert, agile and always 'open', in the sense that it takes nothing for granted and finds nothing surprising. It can move very quickly when profitable opportunities present themselves. It's spontaneous rather than deliberate; opportunist, rather than goal-focused; and tactical, rather than strategic.

It has no particular place to go, no ideal outcome to aspire to.

Just as the RC approach to injustice focuses on real injustices in real societies, rather than on institutional imperfections, so the LFP approach to business focuses on real opportunities rather than strategic coherence and its ability to exploit such opportunities when they appear.

The ultimate objective of an LFP company is always to preserve and strengthen the Gemba (the organization) and so to become a magnet for good people. It sees itself as an ecosystem, as a community of modules staffed by good people and a space where these good people can do interesting, challenging and fulfilling work. LFP companies tend to rank highly in qualitative league tables of environmental and social responsibility (based on perceptions rather than on Key Performance Indicators) and to acquire reputations for being fair, ethical and consistent. But this is not because they're on a mission. Such reputations are by-products of their pragmatism. They value them, nonetheless, because they know that without them, they will find it harder to attract and retain able employees and loyal suppliers and customers.

Its pragmatism and its desire to be able to attract and keep good people leads the LFP company into fuzzy, emotional areas that management theorists have tended to steer well clear of. It acknowledges the constraint imposed by market expectations and the need to keep its cost of capital relatively low, but believes that the best way to do this is to ensure the Gemba Power of its self-adjusting modules remains high and active.

In a retreat from rationalism that would horrify more conventional managers, the managers of LFP companies are interested in emotions and the quality of happiness.

They are aware of the statistical minefields they're entering when they seek enlightenment from happiness indices, but they are also aware of the inadequacies of the conventional assumption that the sum of human happiness can be expressed in money terms. And, being pragmatists, they prefer to rely on fuzzy, equivocal numbers that address the real issue – why good people leave for lower paid jobs and are happier – than on clear, unequivocal numbers that describe an imperfect proxy for the real issue.

They would rather be roughly right, than precisely wrong.

If happiness measures have done nothing else, they've revealed the scale of the imperfection of the money proxy for happiness.

In a report on the nation's wellbeing published in November 2012, the UK's Office for National Statistics (ONS) revealed that people became happier as the UK economy shrank. Life satisfaction scores from the World Database of Happiness, run at Erasmus University in Rotterdam, fell as the economy began to shrink in 2007, but rose as the economy contracted sharply in 2008–09. Then, as GDP picked up slightly, life satisfaction scores fell.[6]

The ONS also measures 'Real Household Actual Income' (RHAI), which accounts for the effect of ultra-low interest rates and increases in social benefits and reductions in taxes that are automatic when the economy contracts. It also attempts to quantify the impact of free healthcare and education on wellbeing. RHAI continued to rise in 2008–09 as life satisfaction scores rose.

The United Nations' international Human Development Index is based on life expectancy and educational achievement as well as income. The

Organization for Economic Co-operation and Development (OECD) has a Better Life Initiative that allows online users to customise a country's rating to reflect the importance people attach to such variables as housing, civic engagement, safety and community.

The Economist Intelligence Unit's 'Global Liveability Index' ranks the world's major cities according to non-economic measures, such as stability, health-care, culture and environment, education and infrastructure.

Lord O'Donnell, former head of the British Civil Service, chairs a commission on well-being run by the Legatum Institute: 'You have to be very careful when using measures, such as RHAI ... But it's a lot better than GDP. It's about trying to look at the right things ... We're at the start of the process, but it will end up being pretty transformational on the way in which we conduct public policy.'[6]

This shift of focus from income, wealth and material well-being to happiness, contentment and psychological or spiritual well-being, seems likely to lead to a re-balancing of the machine or community dualism that has shaped the management debate for a century.

---

[1] 'The Management Century': *Harvard Business Review*, November 2012.

[2] *Steve Jobs*: Little, Brown, 2011.

[3] 'Tim Cook's Freshman Year: The Apple CEO Speaks': *Bloomberg Businessweek*, December 6, 2012.

[4] *China's Management Revolution: Spirit, Land, Energy*: Palgrave Macmillan, 2011.

[5] *The Idea of Justice*: Allen Lane, 2009.

[6] 'Squeezed Households are Happier, Find Statisticians': *Financial Times*, November 21, 2012.

Chapter 10

Building an LFP organization

When Stone Age peoples bartered flint axeheads for spear tips made of sting-ray barbs with an inland tribe, and then sold the axeheads for more spears than they'd paid for them to another tribe that lived between them and the coast, they did not know they were living in the Pleistocene epoch or engaging in arbitrage. They were just doing what seemed logical in the circumstances in which they lived.

Many managers who had never heard of VUCA before reading this book will recognize the phenomena it stands for (Volatility, Uncertainty, Complexity, Ambiguity). Some readers may even recognize in their own organizations some of the characteristics of what is called in earlier chapters the Light Footprint organization. Managers are always adapting and experimenting, insofar as they are free to do so, always trying new things in response to new circumstances. The world has been getting progressively more VUCA-oriented for decades. It would be astonishing if there had been no adaptation to it at all.

The aim of this book is to help managers makes sense of the modern business world and their own and their organizations' place within it, by gathering together some of the glitches, oddities, enigmas, puzzles, paradoxes and incongruities into a new VUCA environment and describing in very general terms the kind of organization likely to survive and thrive in it.

The LFP organization is not one of the 'hopeful monsters' to which Richard Goldschmidt attributed the emergence of new species in his 1940 book, *The Material Basis of Evolution*. It's very similar to a conventional organization and at first glance is indistinguishable from it.

In this final chapter, we will see how managers can begin to effect the micromutations that can change conventional organizations into LFP organizations. Before that, however, it is worth recalling the business case for the LFP approach and why the modern military and recent management innovations in China are instructive precedents.

The case for LFP

The main argument in this book consists of five linked conjectures that can be summarized as follows:

1.The world in which the business and military domains co-exist and overlap is undergoing a fundamental change, equivalent to a phase transition, characterized by the advent of the four VUCA qualities: Volatile, Uncertain, Complex, Ambiguous.

2.The military and business are both subject to the same competitive dynamics; both are engaged in evolutionary arms races.

3.The military is under more competitive pressure than business (the downside is much higher) and has the time and money to think more deeply about the future. It is not surprising, therefore, that it recognized the advent of, and began adapting to, VUCA earlier than business.

4.Modern capitalist China was born right at the dawn of the VUCA age and its companies and management approach are, therefore, like the military, at a more advanced stage of adaptation to the VUCA world than western companies and the western management approach.

5.Ergo, managers wishing to re-frame how they think about the future for business could do worse than look at the adaptive solutions to VUCA conditions the military and Chinese managers have adopted.

Although western managers can learn from the military and from China, business is not war, and the context for business, although being rendered more homogeneous by globalization, was not the same in China after Deng Xiaoping's 'opening' in 1978 as in the West.

These two presages are suggestive, not prescriptive. This is not a 'how to' book. Managers must decide for themselves what lessons they can learn from these military and Chinese precedents. The aim in the rest of this chapter is to give them some pointers.

Acknowledge and diagnose

The first step towards adaptation is to acknowledge that the world has changed and it is incumbent on managers in both the public and private sectors to adapt. If you agree with John Kotter that the greatest challenge today is 'how to stay competitive amid constant turbulence and disruption' (see Chapter 3), become a VUCA believer. Think VUCA. See the world through a VUCA lens. There's evidence of VUCA everywhere for eyes looking for it. What was once strange, odd or plain weird, will begin to make some kind of sense to the VUCA-attuned mind. Look at your own organization and ask yourself if it is 'VUCA-fit'. If you are persuaded that LFP is the way to go, ask yourself how close your organization is to becoming LFP.

To aid your self-diagnosis, consider how well your organization matches up to the following checklist of LFP qualities. Remember that what were formerly strengths may be weaknesses in the VUCA world, and vice versa.

1. Guiding vision

The leader must personify the company and connect with its essence or brand. He or she is a 'strategus', the commander-in-chief of an army, but not a 'strategist', in the modern sense of the word. The leader carries the founder's vision, or initial intent, and guides the organization towards it with persistence and tactical moves.

This guiding vision can take many forms. Good examples include the US Army's 'protect America' vision, Deng Xiaoping's 'to get rich is glorious' vision of a prosperous China and Martin Luther King's 'I have a dream ...' speech. There is also Jack Kennedy's 'I believe that this nation should commit itself to achieving the goal, before this decade is out, of landing a man on the Moon, and returning him safely to the Earth' and Steve Jobs's aesthetic vision, that 'simplicity is the ultimate sophistication'.

The leader's guiding vision isn't confined to the organization. It is a vision of an organization in a context or an environment. In the above examples, for instance, the visions are, respectively, of an America surrounded by enemies; grinding poverty in China after the Great Leap Forward; racism in America; America's 'space race' with the USSR; and the importance of great design in a competitive consumer durables market.

A necessary feature of a guiding vision today is an acceptance of the need to adapt to a relatively new VUCA environment. The leader, from his or her vantage point above the 'Gemba' (organization), is best-placed to recognize the advent of the VUCA world, and has the main responsibility to ensure the organization adapts to it.

As noted in Chapter 4, some of China's company leaders have grasped this challenge. They see their environment as being in a state of more or less permanent flux. This is partly because of the central role that movement plays in the *I Ching*, Daoism and Confucianism, but it also reflects a real fluidity and turbulence in the Chinese and, increasingly, the wider business environment.

Instead of devising and implementing 'strategies', Chinese managers keep shifting distributions of weight and emphasis. Business rules are derived from Chinese social rules, such as the Confucian *li* (proper behaviour), but must be applied to a fluid and constantly changing context.

Chinese managers also have guiding visions, but they're fuzzy. The fuzziness of vision and the turbulence of the environment leads to periods of relatively frenetic movement interspersed by periods of relative calm. Chinese managers value action and patience. But the patience is aggressive, it is the patience of a sprinter waiting for the starting gun.

Leaders exert power over modules mainly through their control over inputs of each module's resources, including human resources (see below). Therefore, they tend to be much more intimately involved than their counterparts at conventional organizations in training and discipline.

Self-test
Has your leader articulated a 'guiding vision'? If so, is it fuzzy enough to guide (rather than direct), or is it too fuzzy to give a useful sense of direction to your modules or decision units?

2. Modular Gemba
The most obvious structural difference between a conventional, and an LFP company is the latter's modular organization. Changing from a traditional functional, departmental, 'siloed' organization to a loose alliance of largely autonomous, multi-disciplinary teams may seem at first sight a formidable challenge, fraught with risk.

But although such a transformation is far from easy, it may not be as formidable or risky in practice as it appears to be in theory. Experience with Accelerated Zero-Based Budgeting projects (AZBB: see Chapter 8) has shown that informal, unofficial modules, known as Decision Units (DUs) in AZBB, operate within most conventional organizations. When HR people talk routinely to finance staff, for example, they are effectively working as the specialist members of a cross-functional team similar to the Operation Hit Back team assembled by Sheila Regan (see Chapter 5).

It's not a huge or a particularly risky step to recognize these teams formally (following their identification during an AZBB project perhaps), to 'empower' them with a high degree of autonomy and to encourage them to assemble the multi-disciplinary skills they need to undertake high value-added projects.

The main advantage of such a modular structure is that feelings of comradeship and shared destiny (and the acknowledgement that comes with such feelings of reciprocal obligations) that endow a company with Gemba (organizational) power, but which tend to dissipate, as the organization grows, re-emerge within the modules.

Re-igniting and retaining Gemba Power in this way becomes more and more important as the organization becomes 'lighter'.

The shift to a modular structure has implications for the style of leadership. 'Empowered' modules manage and modify themselves. Once they are formally recognized, therefore, they must be given a free rein, or at any rate, a freer rein than the same people would have in conventional integrated organizations. They need less direction and management. Too much management may erode the Gemba Power that emerges spontaneously from the comradeship within modules.

Light footprint organizations need light-touch management. The consensual style of leadership that has emerged in China is an instructive model for LFP leadership (see Chapter 4).

Three millennia of imperial rule in China have imprinted the shape of hierarchy on the national psyche. The leader is a key component of a well-ordered Confucian society but the position brings with it certain obligations. A ruler's mandate is conditional on his or her good behaviour. The people acknowledge the need for a ruler to guide them, and make those decisions only the leader can make, but they retain the right to disobey badly behaved leaders.

This conditional acceptance of the leader's power is of particular relevance to the modular LFP organization because modules *think*: they couldn't be self-managing and self-directing if they did not. And, as the CEO of a large multinational corporation put it to the author, 'Thinking is the beginning of disobeying.'

The conditional mandate has two other consequences.

First, leaders recognize the claims of employees on the value they help to create and honour the unwritten contract between a leader and the led that, if the latter work hard to enrich the former, the former will give them something back.

Second, although the leader makes the decisions that reach the top after the application of the principle of subsidiarity (see Chapter 5), he or she will only do so after long discussions with advisers. It is the way China is governed. Decisions to change the direction of policy are only taken after lengthy debates of leaked proposals.

The modules think for themselves – the leader thinks for the whole organization. That is why Chinese company leaders typically have a well-staffed, well-resourced private office (*dong ban*).

Self-test
Have you identified the hidden or unacknowledged modular structure of your organization? What can you do to strengthen and 'empower' the modules and establish an appropriate relationship between each module and the centre?

3. Yin and Yang
Although many of their managers do their best to disguise the fact, conventional companies are basically mechanical – just engines for creating value for their shareholders. LFP companies are basically dialectical: they are constantly balancing, reconciling, trading-off and negotiating. They are machines and communities; they are centralized and de-centralized; high-tech and simple; fast and reflective; opportunistic and persistent; hopeful and fearful.

The have what Scott Fitzgerald said was, 'the test of a first-rate intelligence ... the ability to hold two opposing ideas in mind at the same time and still retain the ability to function'.

LFP companies thrive on such tensions and on the controversies and argument they generate, because they provide energy and they lead to clarity, consensus and what Chris Argyris calls 'internal commitment' (see Chapter 8). It may be simpler to regard companies as machines and employees as cogs and ratchets, but it's unrealistic. Treating people as cogs in a machine is naïve at the best of times, and in a VUCA world, where tiny causes can have enormous consequences, it can be disastrous.

The US Navy SEALs who shot Osama bin Laden were self-managing and highly motivated. Each was committed to his comrades, to his corps and to his country and his commander-in-chief sitting and watching patiently with his staff in the White House situation room.

That many Chinese managers see employees as more than mere cogs in their machines is evident in their invocations of spiritual powers to explain the company's purpose and elicit 'internal' commitment.

If anything, the Chinese are less religious than westerners but, in the West, the engines of business run in a material world separate from the spiritual world and are driven by commercial imperatives that have nothing to do with the spiritual and philosophical aspects of human personalities.

LFP companies know that a company adapted to a VUCA environment is as much a community of people as a machine for creating value.

Self-test

How well balanced is the organization? Is it too much of a machine or too much of a community? Are paradox and tension welcomed and seen as a source of creativity, or are efforts being made to eliminate differences and remove tensions? Does the organization accommodate and value the spiritual side of human beings?

4. Collaboration

LFP company leaders also recognize that the human communities that are their companies nest within – and are parts of – wider communities of interest and of allegiance.

No organization is an island. All operate within other communities and their fates depend, to a large extent, on the quality of their relationships with these other communities. LFP organizations see, in their business and supply chain friendships, virtually infinite scope for their own growth and development.

They understand the power of reciprocity and the value of customer and employee loyalty. They also recognize the value of reputations: being a good customer, a good supplier, a good employer and a good ally or partner.

Feng Jun, founder of the Huaqi PC products company, and creator of the aigo brand (a sponsor of the McLaren Formula 1 racing team) is one of China's new generation of high-tech entrepreneurs. He likes to be known as 'six wins Feng', because he is committed to running his company in ways that reconcile the reasonable interests of six constituencies: customers, distributors, employees, suppliers, the company itself and society at large (see Chapter 4).

LFP organizations have the same sense of reciprocal obligation and inter-dependence. They try hard to cultivate reputations for being trustworthy and are predisposed to trust others.

In the new VUCA version of the game of business, where transaction costs are minimal and the economics of partnerships and alliances are becoming increasingly attractive, LFP companies trust on first encounters and then play tit-for-tat (see Chapter 7).

Partnerships are particularly attractive to LFP companies, because they allow the organization to extend its scope and reach, without adding mass. ARM Holdings dominates the world market for mobile phone processors with its high code-density, low power consumption RISC chips, but its substance consists mostly of partnerships (see Chapter 7).

Being as light as possible is a core value for LFP companies. They share President Obama's view of alliances, coalitions and the use of proxies:

that a footprint shared, is a footprint halved (see Chapter 7). They also subscribe to Buckminster Fuller's notion of 'ephemeralisation'; doing 'more and more with less and less, until eventually you can do everything with nothing'.

LFP organizations are open to all influences, but are in thrall to none. There's no 'not invented here' prejudice. Any ideas that are relevant, any tools that are useful are adopted without reference to their origins. LFP managers share Deng's view: if the cat can catch mice, its colour and provenance are immaterial. They are as willing to learn from the military and China as they are to learn from the *Harvard Business Review*.

Self-test

Could your organization be lighter? Does it prefer acquisitions to alliances, joint-ventures and partnerships? Are its relationships built mostly on trust or mostly on formal agreements and detailed contracts? What decision rules would the organization employ in an iterated Prisoners' Dilemma tournament?

5. Unmanned

During the early stages of the microelectronics revolution, a joke had some currency for a while about a 'microchip company' that was so successful it had to move into smaller premises. LFP managers, with their commitment to lightness and doing more with less, might find it hard to see the funny side. Moving into smaller premises, without sacrificing scope or reach, might seem to them to be quite a reasonable aspiration.

An aspect of the LFP organization's commitment to lightness is its technophilia: its hunger for the new, the latest and the 'next big thing'. LFP managers see robotics and automation as contributions to lightness, just as President Obama sees drones as an integral part of his 'light footprint' military doctrine. They tend to be 'early adopters' of new technologies and always to be on the look out for new ways to do more with less.

In a fast-changing world, early adopters are 'early adapters'. They experiment with and adapt new technologies and keep their ears to the ground (as well as their eyes on the technology producers), to keep abreast of what other experimenters and adapters are up to.

When Steve Jobs acquired control of what became Pixar, he wanted to widen the markets for the company's image computer and rendering software by producing cheaper versions. He believed people find 'clever new ways to use tools . . . the inventor never imagined' (see Chapter 5). LFP managers keep their ears to the ground, because they realize that, as science-fiction author William Gibson put it, 'the street finds its own uses for technology'.

Many LFP technophiles have voracious appetites for science fiction and particularly for near-future sci-fi by Gibson (inventor of the term 'cyberspace') and other so-called 'cyberpunk' authors such as Neal Stephenson. By imagining the future within the 'cloud' or the 'fifth domain', as the Pentagon calls the Internet, these writers provide an antidote of a kind to what Alvin Toffler called 'Future Shock'.

Regular doses of sci-fi will help prepare LFP technophiles for the 'big one', expected in the next three decades: the event horizon of what is known as the 'technological singularity', the emergence of true artificial intelligence (see Chapter 5).

Self-test
Is your organization techno 'phile', or 'phobe'? To what extent is it automated? Is it an early adopter or a reluctant follower? Does the organizational community spend much time discussing the coming 'technological singularity' or reading near-future science fiction books?

6. Data friendly
Before the technological singularity is upon us, some companies are likely to buried under mountains of data growing at an exponential rate. Not so LFP organizations. They will learn to mine 'big data' for commercially valuable information, and filter, distil and edit it into timely, pertinent information for decision-making.

Considerable investment or, as LFP companies may prefer, extensive partnership arrangements, might be required to meet the challenge of 'big data'; namely to extract more useful information more quickly from the deep oceans of data that surround all organizations than your rivals. Sophisticated sets of sensors and access to the best analysts and the latest analytical algorithms will be required.

This is likely to become a very competitive area and the services of data analysis 'gurus', such as Nate Silver, will be much sought after. Silver's recent rise to prominence is another glitch in the matrix, of the kind discussed in Chapter 1. A decade ago it would have been astonishing if a statistician had been included in *Time* magazine's *The World's 100 Most Influential People*, as was Silver in 2009. In the VUCA world it is not surprising that a man who can tease the tiniest nuances of meaning from 'big [and getting bigger by the moment] data', should have become a celebrity.

Silver is like the alchemists of the Enlightenment. He is building the foundations of a new science. The title of his 2012 book, *The Signal and the Noise* (Penguin), neatly captures the essence of the 'big data' challenge.

Self-test

Is your organization geared up for 'big data'? Does it have enough sensors and data analysis capability? Can it distil, summarize and edit accurately and quickly enough to ensure decisions are timely and well-informed?

7. In synch

Time, of which there is always too little, and speed, of which there is never enough, are LFP leadership dimensions. The leader has to manage the momentum, establish the rhythm and ensure there is time to gather information, analyse, explain, convince and encourage.

The leader must also keep the organization 'poised': ready to move fast enough, to match the speed of change in the environment. As a UK CEO said years ago when engaged in a major change programme, 'I am more interested in speed than in direction'.

Being able to keep pace with changes in the environment is part of what 'lightness' is for.

In the old days, when Bruce Henderson's 'experience curve' was the 'big thing', mass and market share were not only the spoils of the last victory, they were also a competitive advantage for the next battle. 'Economies of scale' were everything. You had to be market leader or a strong challenger, or you were dead in the water.

In the VUCA business world, mass and the inertia that comes with it are liabilities.

The problem for the conventional organization in the VUCA world is not its lack of speed. Given time, a massive organization can build up to a very high speed. It is nimbleness, agility and the ability to change course quickly, at a moment's notice, that matters. It is precisely in these areas where the LFP organization excels. Racing car designer Colin Chapman, founder of Lotus, is said to have been dismayed if his cars didn't fall apart a yard over the finishing line: it 'must be over-engineered' he would think, 'Where can we take off weight?'

It is speed around the track, rather than speed in a straight line, that wins motor races, and that is about acceleration (determined by the ratio of power to weight), braking power and handling. On its debut at the 23km Nordschleife track at the Nürburgring in May 1962, the tiny Lotus 23 led a field of Porsches, Aston Martins and Ferraris – some of which had four times the power of the Lotus – by 27 seconds at the end of the first lap. The Lotus, driven by Jim Clark, extended its lead each lap until the track dried. Clark was overcome by exhaust fumes on lap 12 and crashed.

Acceleration and manoeuvrability are the winning qualities in the VUCA world, especially in the wet when grip is minimal, you don't know exactly where you're going and all the corners are blind. Metaphorically, it's always raining or about to rain in the VUCA world. It's slippery. Traction is hard to find.

LFP companies are 'in synch' with the rhythms as well as the speed and turbulence of the VUCA environment. As Chinese entrepreneurs have realized, although there is no equilibrium to adapt to in the VUCA business world, there are discernible and predictable cycles and seasons. Spring follows Winter. Summer follows Spring. Fruit ripens in the Autumn (see Chapter 4). LFP managers 'synch in' with these environmental rhythms so that the organization is ready when a season turns or a cycle switches direction.

Self-test
What can your organization do to shed mass and make itself nimble enough to negotiate the twists and turns of the VUCA environment?

What can it do to synchronize itself more closely with the seasons and cycles of the environment?

8. The new natural

Business organizations and management styles emerge – they are not deliberately designed. But they emerge in particular places, at particular times. They carry the imprint of those places and times throughout the rest of their lives. To paraphrase the late Stephen Jay Gould, 'each organization and management style is a quirky mass of imperfections, working well enough (often admirably); a jury-rigged set of adaptations, built of curious parts, made available by past histories in different contexts'.[1] Among the 'curious parts' of the style emerging in China is the 'borrowed' management style that emerged in the context of mid-19th century America.

The 'jury-rigged set of adaptations' isn't assembled randomly. The viable set is selected by the environment. The VUCA environment is significantly different from all pre-VUCA environments and can be expected to select a significantly different set of adaptations. This will lead to a cull of adaptations that worked well enough in the past but are disadvantageous in the VUCA environment.

Company leaders should ask themselves which in their existing sets of adaptations, including those adaptations specific to their own companies as well as those that comprise the conventional wisdom, would not be selected if they were starting again from scratch and knew nothing of the organization's history and endowments.

From an understanding of the VUCA environment, a rough idea can be derived of the new 'natural' organization, of the set of qualities most likely to thrive in that environment. Comparing this picture of the new natural companies with their existing organizations allows them to act like Darwin's pigeon breeders and artificially select and de-select advantageous and disadvantageous qualities.

It's like designing a new Swiss Army Knife with its numerous tools and gadgets. You would not want a tool for extracting stones from horses' hooves in your VUCA knife but a USB memory stick might be handy.

President Obama designed a new military knife when he replaced the Colin Powell doctrine (namely, only deploy US forces under conditions of overwhelming superiority) with the 'light footprint' doctrine. He selected, and de-selected: in with drones, cyber weapons, special forces, and proxies, out with the big battalions and shock and awe (see Chapter 2).

Xavier Niel designed a new mobile telephony knife in 2009 when his company, Free, won a mobile licence from the French regulator: its ISP customers helped finance the construction, at record speed, of the lightest mobile network the regulations allowed. Free signed a six-year roaming deal with Orange and co-opted its wi-fi 'hotspot' network to help serve the data needs of mobile customers. Niel then shocked the market with rock-bottom prices (see Chapter 1).

Self-test
Which of your organization's assumptions, conventions, habits and pre-dispositions are inhibiting the change to an LFP, VUCA-adapted organization? And which are facilitating it? How can the latter be encouraged and the former discouraged?

9. Precise and tactical
In a VUCA world, you can't afford to be too wedded to a plan or to be burdened by an excessively detailed vision of your destination. You need to be flexible, and flexibility is inversely proportional to the rigidity and clarity of your vision for the future.

That is why some Chinese managers have 'fuzzy' visions and juggle with several opportunities at once. They are opportunistic – their next steps will depend on which of the various opportunities 'goes live' first.

A vision is necessary to steer in roughly the right direction, but the accuracy of the course is less important than the alertness of the look-outs.

It's the same with the LFP organization.

But the characteristic 'fuzziness' of an LFP organization's vision is in sharp contrast to the clinical precision of all its tactical moves. Lightness both requires and allows precisely targeted, low-impact missions. When something has to be done, do it quickly, and don't make waves.

It's a different, lower-level kind of corporate action. The leader gives the green light but the planning and the mission itself are executed at the modular level. An Accelerated Zero-Based Budgeting (AZBB, see Chapter 8) project can be useful here, by providing a space and pretext for conversations between the leadership and the modules that would not, in the normal course of events, occur.

There are two other features of high precision hit-and-run strikes that LFP company leaders should bear in mind.

The first is that, because these tactical moves are supposed to be precise and low-impact, any collateral damage that does occur will be very visible, and often controversial, after the event. There is less risk of, and less actual, collateral damage than equivalents in business of 'big battalion' warfare but the non-combatant deaths, particularly of young children, that do occur are felt more keenly and when reported in the media cause more reputational damage.

The second feature of fast, high-precision hit-and-run raids that LFP leaders should bear in mind is that the raids rely heavily on the element of surprise. In the past, companies tended to be open about their strategies because leaders wanted employees to 'buy in' to them and investment analysts made judgments about the value of a listed company partly on the basis of how impressed they were by its declared strategy.

LFP companies don't have strategies in the normal sense, and have to play their tactical cards close to their chests. If they didn't, they would lose that vital element of surprise. If Osama bin Laden had known about Operation Neptune Spear beforehand, he could have left the Abbottabad compound or made arrangements that would have frustrated the raid. Special forces teams are agile, well-equipped and very well trained, but they're small. They stand little chance of success if the enemy knows where and when they plan to strike.

Self-test
How precisely are your organization's tactical moves targeted? Are they well-planned and accurately timed? What efforts are made to ensure

they do not leak out beforehand? Are efforts made to assess and mini-mize likely collateral damage?

10. Enlightened

LFP company leaders are attuned to the *zeitgeist*, to the spirit of the times, the public mood. They are clear about their company's purpose and about its role in the societies in which it operates. They know what's expected of them. They acknowledge their need for legitimacy, and the goodwill of ordinary people.

They recognize that in the second decade of the 21st century, as the world economy still struggles to regain its strength following the trau-mas of the 2007–08 banking crisis, 'business' has a legitimacy defi-ciency. They see it as in the interests of everyone, including their share-holders, that they should help to re-build public trust and confidence in business and in business people.

Like the Chinese entrepreneur Feng Jun with his 'six wins' view of busi-ness, they see the company as one of a group of constituencies, includ-ing society at large, that depend on one another and have a mutual interest in and claims on the value created by business.

But they are pragmatic, rather than idealistic. They don't want to change the world, they simply want to make it better insofar as it is in their power to do so.

They're good with numbers and they recognize their need to master the challenges of 'big data'. But they know numbers don't tell the whole story. They acknowledge the technical weaknesses of measures of well-being and happiness but they do not dismiss them for that reason. They take the pragmatist's view: it's better to be roughly right than precisely wrong.

Self-test

How responsive is the organization to public mood and to human, as opposed to business, needs and hungers? To what extent would you say it is aware of, and integrated with the societies and cultures within which it operates?

Step by step

The second step towards adaptation is to recognize that you cannot, and must not try, to do it all at once. Adaptation proceeds through a series of micromutations not 'hopeful monster' macromutations.

Set the course, deploy your four-letter acronym tools (see Chapter 8) and prepare to act. An AZBB exercise is a good starting point. It will be self-financing, will take no hostages to fortune if you decide to do nothing else and should reveal the components of the modular organization lying hidden in your traditional hierarchical structure (see Chapter 8).

If you feel that a formal switch to a modular, LFP organization is too radical or too risky, you could try Kotter's hybrid system and recruit a 'strategy network' of volunteers that operates alongside and in concert with a traditional hierarchical system (see Chapter 3). Kotter's model is a patch on the existing system but he is on the button with the problem: 'The 21st century will force us all to evolve toward a fundamentally new form of organization.'

Plan bottom-up projects, focus on a few key levers, conduct pilots and 'feel the stones' by trial and error as you cross the river. Find out what works for your organization. Support unexpected, but interesting, developments that appear to lead in roughly the right direction. Go with the flow.

Keep managing. There are no solutions, just constant adaptation to the VUCA environment. Remain true to the over-arching principle of lightness. Adopt Colin Chapman's approach to race car design: keep shedding weight until you have just enough. Favour partnerships over acquisitions. Automate. Keep alert. Move quickly and precisely. Let your Gemba do your thinking.

In praise of lightness

Lightness is a primary virtue in the VUCA world in every area and in all walks of life: lightness of warfare, lightness of industry and commerce, of government and institutions, including companies. Treading lightly on nature, societies and communities; on people's dreams and memories.

The quality of lightness should on no account be mistaken for such qualities as transient, ephemeral or superficial. The impression left by Neil Armstrong's boot on the moon on July 21, 1969 was the lightest footprint ever made by a human adult, and it's still there.

---

[1] Based on a passage in *The Flamingo's Smile*: W. W. Norton, 1985.

Index

3-D printing 80
Abbott, James 41
Abbottabad 41, 42, 97, 98, 114, 187
Accelerated Zero-Based Budgeting (AZBB) xi, 4,
    146, 177, 187
Accenture 12, 103
Acorn Computers 111–113
Activity-Based Costing (ABC) 15, 139, 143, 149
Adams, John 51
Adaptive Strategic Planning Process (ASPP) 146
Adobe 91, 93, 95
Advent Chamber Orchestra 101
A Far Cry orchestra 101
agency costs 110, 154
Agha-Soltan, Neda 52
agile combat aircraft (ACA) 119–121, 137, 151
Ahmadinejad, Mahmoud 51
Al-Jazeera 52
al-Qaeda 36
Aldrich 8
Alexander 101
Alexander, General Keith 38
Alibaba 70
Amazon 131
American Association for the Advancement of
    Science 47
Ames Research Center 81
Amsterdam Sinfonietta 101
Ansoff, Igor 11
Apple 3, 88–95, 99, 104, 123, 137, 162, 164
Apple II 61
Arcot 6
Argyris, Chris 153, 154, 179
Arizona Chamber Orchestra 101
ARM Holdings 111–113, 180
arms race 30, 31, 33-35, 37, 40, 43, 78, 80, 174
Armstrong, Neil 190
ARPANET 34
Ars Nova Chamber Orchestra 101
Arthur Andersen 12
Arthur D. Little 9, 11
artificial intelligence 37, 81, 82, 130, 182
Aston Martin 184
A. T. Kearney 10, 104
Australian Chamber Orchestra 101
Autorité de régulation des communications
    électroniques et des postes (ARCEP) 19
Axelrod, Robert 105-109
Aznar, José María 51

Baker, George 8
Battle of Bannockburn 30
Battle of Hampton Roads 31, 43
Battle of Plassey 6, 7
Battle of the Golden Spurs 30
Battle of the Somme 115
Battle of Tsushima 32
Beckwith, Charlie 41
Beijing Olympics 64
Belzberg brothers 14
Ben Ali, President 52
Bentham, Jeremy 166
Berger, Roland 12
Bergius process 34
Better Life Initiative 172
Biden, Joe 42, 97
big data xii, 130–132, 134, 182, 183, 188
Bill of Rights 141
bin Laden, Osama 41, 42, 97, 114, 123, 179, 187
Black Hole of Calcutta 6, 7
Blair, Dennis 128
Bloching, Björn 130, 131
Bo Xilai 25
Bollen, Johan 83
Bonaparte, Napoleon 161
Bond, James 41
Bonn-Rhein-Sieg University of Applied Sciences 9
Booz, Allen & Hamilton 11, 103
Boren, David 45
Boston Consulting Group 11, 157
Boulton, Matthew 102
Bouygues Telecom 19
Bower, Marvin 10, 11
Branson, Sir Richard 21
Braun, Wernher von 34
Brennan, John 97
Brimm, Michael 162
Brom, Shlomo 116
Budgeting and Accounting Act 141
Bureau of the Budget 141
Bush, George W. 36, 45, 78
Business Process Re-engineering (BPR) 15, 139,
    140, 143, 147

Cambridge *keretsu* 112
Carroll, Dave 82, 83
Carter, James (Jimmy) 143
Caulfield, Holden 94
CCTV 68

Central Intelligence Agency (CIA) 45, 123
Centre for the Study of Existential Risk 82
China Europe International Business School
　(CEIBS) ix, 8
Clark, Jim 184
Clausewitz, Carl von 11, 29, 84
Clinton, Hillary 97
Clive, Robert 6, 7
Champy, James 139
Chandler, Alfred 5, 8, 110, 111
Change Management Program (CMP) 147
Chapman, Colin 184, 189
Cheung Kong Graduate School of Business
　(CKGSB) ix, 8, 9
Cheung Kong (Holdings) 9
Chindits 41
Chinese Communist Party (CCP) 25, 62, 67, 68,
　73, 98
Christian Science Monitor 54
Chrysler 158
Churchill, Sir Winston 41
Cisco Systems 47
Citicorp 8
Coase, Ronald 110, 111
Cohen, Jared 52
collateral damage 76, 77, 79, 88, 97, 115, 147, 187,
　188
Commandos 41
Commodore PET 2001 61
Common Sense 51
Compaq 124
Competence Value Map (CVM) 146
Complex Adaptive Systems 3, 48, 49, 135–137
complexity 3, 46, 47, 56, 57, 79, 85, 120, 124,
　135–138, 143, 144, 146, 173
Confucius 25, 66, 166
Condorcet, Nicolas de 166
Congress 31, 32, 43
Continuous Change Management Program
　(CCMP) 147
Cook, Tim 162
corporate social responsibility (CSR) 15, 22, 169
Cresap, McCormick & Paget 11
Crockett, Horace G. 10
Cumberland 31, 43
Cultural Revolution 61
Cumnock 8
Customer Relationship Management (CRM) 15,
　130
Cyber-punk 89
cyber weapons 3, 40, 43, 45, 77, 78, 84, 97, 186
Czechoslovak Radio Symphony Orchestra 100
Dao de Ching 65
Daoism 2, 3, 29, 65–67, 70, 95, 125, 176
Darwin, Charles 4, 29, 30, 43, 185
data friendly 3, 128, 129, 134, 138, 155, 182
Dawkins, Richard 13, 138
decision package 148

decision unit 148, 149, 153, 176, 177
Dell 124
Dell, Michael 19
Delta Force 41
Deming, Edwards 15, 16
Deng Xiaoping 61–64, 70, 72, 174, 175, 181
Denning, Steve 22
Department of Homeland Security 128
Derwent Capital Markets 83
Descartes, Renée 26
Dickens, Charles 139
Diderot, Denis 26
digital hub 91–93, 95
Disney 89, 90, 95, 104
Disney, Roy 89
dong ban (chairman's office) 74, 98, 164, 178
Donilon, Tom 97
dot.com bubble 91, 130, 131, 138
Dow Jones 84
Dreadnought 33, 40
drones (UAVs) 3, 35–38, 43, 45, 77, 115
Drucker, Peter 99, 157
Duqu 40
Dylan, Bob 93
Dynamic Competence Value Map (DCVM) 146

East Coast Chamber Orchestra 101
East, Warren 113, 131
eBay 109
Economist Intelligence Unit 172
Efficient Market Hypothesis 167
Einstein, Albert 88
Eisner, Michael 90
empowerment 98, 121, 124, 151, 153, 154, 162
Endo, Isao 59, 126
English East India Company (EEIC) 6, 7, 110
Enigma Code 34
Enron 12
ephemeralisation 181
Erasmus University 171
Ericsson, John 34
Estienne, Jean Baptiste 34
Estrada, Joseph 51
ETH Zurich 131
European Network and Information Security
　Agency (ENISA) 38
Evans, Jonathan 84
Existential threats 81, 82
experience curve 14, 15, 157, 183

F35 37
Facebook 50–53, 82, 131
Farrell, Matt 40
Feng Jun 72, 73, 146, 161, 180, 188
Ferrari 184
Fifer, Julian 101
fifth domain 82
Financial Times 8, 23

Fink, Dietmar 9
FireWire 91
Fischer–Tropsch process 34
Fitzgerald, Scott 179
Flame 40
fly-by-wire 119, 137
Ford 158
Ford, Gerald 45
Ford, Henry 19
Ford, Henry II 158
Foreign Policy 77
Formula 1 31, 119, 180
Fortune 45
Fortune 500 17, 18, 103
Foxbot 80
Foxconn 80
fragmented authoritarianism 67
Franklin, Benjamin 26, 88
Free 18–21, 186
Fry, Robert 41, 42, 78, 123
Fukushima 56
Fukuyama, Francis 105
Fuld, Dick 42
Fuller, Buckminster 181

Galbraith, J. K. 157
Gates, Robert 45, 97
Gauss 40
Gemba 3, 25, 59, 67, 85, 126, 127, 134, 137, 151, 170, 171, 176, 177, 189
General Atomics 36
General Conference on Weights and Measures 47
General Electric 12, 14, 82, 138
Ghandi, Mahatma 161
Gibson, William 89, 182
Glass–Steagall Act 10
Gleick, James 47
Global Liveability Index 172
Global Times 54
Goldschmidt, Richard 173
Goldsmith, Sir James 14
Google 21, 81, 84, 131
Gould, Stephen Jay 185
Government Communications Headquarters (GCHQ) 38
Great Leap Forward 62, 88, 175
Green Herald 69
Griffin and Little 9
Griffin, Roger 9
growth share matrix 157
Guibert, Count Jacques Antoine Hippolyte 11
Gulf War 36
Gurkhas 41

Hackman, Richard 100
Hamas 116
Hamel, Gary 15, 22, 168
Hammer, Mike 139

Hanson Trust 14
Harvard Business Review 22, 142
Harvard Business School ix, 1, 7, 8, 10, 15, 23, 57, 107, 145, 153, 181
Harvard University 22, 100
Hastings, Warren 7
Hawthorne experiments 157
Helbing, Dirk 131, 132
Henderson, Bruce 11, 12, 14, 157, 183
H. L. Hunley 33
Hobbes, Thomas 165
hopeful monster 4, 173, 189
Housatonic 33
HTSB group 162
Huaqi 180
Human Development Index 171
Hunley, Horace Lawson 33, 34
Hutchison Whampoa 9

Iacocca, Lee 158
IBM 124
IBM PC 61, 123
Icahn, Carl 14
iChat 161
I Ching 65, 70, 131, 176
iMac 90, 91
INSEAD 162
Institute of National Security Studies 116
Integrated Value Based Management (IVBM) 146
Intel 124, 130
International Federation of Robotics 80
iPad 80, 92, 93
iPhone 80, 93, 95
iPhoto 91
iPod 92, 95, 98
Iraqi Republican Guard 123
Isaacson, Walter 88, 89, 93, 160, 162
iTunes 91
Ive, Sir Jonathan 90, 98

Jacobson, William 23
Jane's All the World's Aircraft 35
Jarvis, Jeff 55
Jasmine Revolution 56
Jefferson, Thomas 26
Jin Dynasty 30
jingzuo (meditation) 70, 161
Jobs, Steve 3, 19, 88–95, 98, 99, 123, 160–162, 164, 175, 182
Johnson, Lyndon 141, 142
Johnson, Thomas 139
Jones Day 10
Justice Department 128

K-Mart 8
kaizen 87
Kant, Immanuel 165
Kaplan, Robert 139

Kaspersky, Eugene 40
Kearney, Andrew 10
Kennedy, Jack 25, 175
Kennedy School 22
Kiechel, Walter 157–159
King, Martin Luther 175
Kirzner, Israel 69
Kissinger, Henry 25
Kotter, John 1, 4, 7, 23, 57–59, 135–137, 175, 189
KPMG 104
Kramer, Mark 22
Kresge 8
Kurzweil, Ray 81, 82

Lampedusa, Giuseppe di 139
Lao Tzu 65, 125, 163
Lasica, J. D. 53
Lasseter, John 90, 95
Ledru-Rollin, Alexandre 161
Legatum Institute 172
Lehman Bothers 42
Leibniz, Gottfried 26, 166
Lenovo 123
li (ritual) 66
Li Chengpeng 54
Li Ka-shing 9
Li Ka-shing Foundation 9
Little, Arthur Dehon 9
Little, Brown 94
little data 132
Live Earth Simulator (LES) 131, 132
Live Free or Die Hard 40
Locke, John 26, 165
logic bomb 38, 39, 43
London Interbank Offer Rate (LIBOR) 24
Long Range Desert Group 41
Long Term Incentive Plan 17, 168
Lorenz, Edward 47, 48
Lotus 184
Lotus 23 184
Lucasfilm 89
Luck, Lars 180
Luther, Martin 50
Lynn, William J. 38
Lyra Vivace Chamber Orchestra 101

Ma Yun (Jack Ma) 69, 70, 73, 161
McAfee, Andrew 47
McGregor, Douglas 157
McKinsey, James O. 10
McKinsey & Company 10–12, 14
Mclaren 180
Macbeth 65
Majestic 32
Mandate of Heaven (*dian ming*) 66, 98
Mandela, Nelson 161
Mandelbrot set 136
Mao Zedong 25, 62, 64

Marakon 14
Marshall Field 10
Marx, Karl 166
Mayo, Elton 157
Merrimack (a.k.a. *C.S.S. Virginia*) 31–33, 40, 43
Merton, Robert 26
Micawber, Wilkins 139
Microsoft 39, 124
Military Intelligence Program (MIP) 128
Mill, John Stuart 166
Mini-Flame 40
Ministry of International Trade and Industry (MITI) 63
MIT Center for Digital Business 47
modular organization 85, 99, 104, 105, 121, 124, 125, 134, 138, 152, 159, 163, 176–178, 187, 189
Moltke, Helmuth von 11
Monitor, U.S.S. 32–34, 43
Monitor Group 22
Montesquieu, Charles-Louis de 26
Montreal Gazette 82
Moore, Gordon 130
Moore's Law 130
Morgan 8
Morgan Guaranty 8
Morgan Stanley 8
Morgenstern, Oskar 11
Morita, Akio 158
Morozov, Evgeny 52
Moses, Mark 37
Moss Kanter, Rosabeth 153
muda (waste) 16, 127, 144
Mullen, Mike 97
Müller-Dofel, Mario 57, 121
Multiple Stakeholder Value Model (MSVM) 146
Multi-Unit Business Enterprise (MUBE) 5, 7, 8, 110, 111
mura (inconsistency) 127
muri (strain) 127
Mutually Assured Destruction (MAD) 30
MySpace 53

Napster 91
National Aeronautics and Space Administration (NASA) 81
NASDAQ 113
Natanz 39, 40, 114
National Intelligence Program (NIP) 128
National People's Congress 66
National Security Agency 38
Navstar-GPS 35
Nawab (nabob) 7, 110
Neumann, John von 11
New America Foundation 77
New Century Chamber Orchestra 101
Newton, Sir Isaac 26
NeXT 90

Niel, Xavier 19–21, 186
Nordschleife 184
Novak, William 158
Nürburgring 184

Obama, Barack xii, 2, 3, 36–38, 42–45, 48, 53, 55, 76–79, 97, 98, 102, 114–116, 132, 137, 180, 181, 186
O'Donnell, Lord Gus 172
Office for National Statistics (ONS) 171
off-shoring 79, 80
Operation Desert Storm 36
Operation Eagle Claw 42, 97
Operation Hit Back 06, 07, 114, 177
Operation Neptune Spear 42, 114, 187
Opium War 6
Oppenheimer, Robert 34
Oracle at Delphi 65, 131
Orange 19, 20, 186
Orange Revolution 51
Organization for Economic Co-operation and Development (OECD) 172
Orpheus Chamber Orchestra 99–101

Paine, Thomas 26, 51
Painter, John 101
Panetta, Leon 45
Paracelsus 129
Parachute Regiment 41
Parker, Graham 100
Pascale, Richard 14, 143
People's Daily 68
Persimfans orchestra 100
pike 30, 31
Pixar 89, 90, 95, 104, 160, 182
Pixar Image Computer 89
Planning-Programming-Budgeting System (PPBS) 141, 142
Polaris 33
Politburo 25, 133
Popper, Sir Karl 130
Porsche 184
Porter, Michael 15, 18, 22, 71, 158, 168
Powell, Colin 41, 45, 115, 137, 186
Prague Chamber Orchestra 100
Prahalad, C.K. 15
Precision Engagement Module 37
precision-guided munitions 34, 115
Predator 36
Price, Huw 82
Prisoners' dilemma 108
psychological contract 124
PwC 84
Pyhrr, Peter 142–144

Ramge, Thomas 130
RasGas 84
Rawls, John 165

Real Household Actual Income (RHAI) 171, 172
realization-focused comparison 166, 170
Reaper 36, 38
Reduced Instruction Set Computer (RISC) 111–113, 180
Rees, Lord 82
Regan, Sheila 86, 87, 114, 177
ren (benevolence) 66
re-shoring 80
Revolutionary Armed Forces of Colombia (FARC) 51
Reyes rendering program 89
Robbins, Anthony 136
Rockefeller 8
Roland Berger xi, xii, 126
Roosevelt, Franklin 25
Rothkopf, David 77
Rousseau, Jean Jacques 165
Royal Air Force (RAF) 35
Rubinstein, Jon 92, 93
Rumsfeld, Donald 41, 45, 132

Salinger, J. D. 94
Sanger, David 77
Sanger, Larry 50
Saudi Aramco 84
Saxby, Sir Robin 111–113
Schein, Edgar 94
Schwenker, Burkhard 57, 121
Scully, John 99
Sea Air Land (SEAL) 41, 97, 114, 179
sea turtles 63, 69
Seifter, Harvey 99, 100
Sen, Amartya 165, 166, 168, 170
Sepoy Mutiny 7
SFR 19
Shakespeare, William 49
Shamoon 84
Shapir, Yiftah 116
Shareholder Value Maximization (SVM) 146, 168, 169
Shockley, William 18
Sichuan earthquake 64
Siemens 39, 114
Silver, Nate 183
Sina Weibo 54
Singularity Institute 82
Singularity University 81
six wins 72, 146, 161, 180, 188
Skype 51, 82
Smith, Adam 14, 26, 166, 167
Smith, Lee 45
Solidarity 51
Sons of Maxwell 82
Sony 93, 158, 164
SoundJam 91, 104
spar torpedo 31, 33
Special Air Service (SAS) 41
Special Boat Service 41

special forces 3, 41–43, 45, 48, 77, 78, 84, 97, 102, 115, 121, 127, 155, 186, 187
Spinoza, Baruch 26
Standard Oil 8
Stephenson, Neal 182
Stern Stewart 14
Stevens, J. P. 8
stirrups 30
Strategic Planning Associates 14
Strategic Planning Process (SPP) 146
Strategus 1, 11, 28, 160, 161, 175
Stuxnet 39, 40, 84, 114
subsidiarity 85, 159, 178
Sun Tszu 29, 31, 41, 43, 65
Suraj-ud-Dowlah 6

tai chi 66, 70, 147, 161
tai chi, jinyu (keeping silent) 70, 161
tai chi quan (shadow boxing) 70
Taliban 36
Tallinn, Jaan 82
Tandy TRS-80 61
Tarot 65
Taylor, Frederick 14, 157
technological singularity 81, 82, 130, 182
Terminator 77
Texas Instruments 140, 142
The Economist 38
The Matrix 17
theory X 157
theory Y 157
Thiel, Peter 82
Time 183
tit for tat (TFT) 108, 109, 163, 180
Toffler, Alvin 182
Tognetti, Richard 101
Toshiba 92, 93
total quality management (TQM) 15, 16
Township and Village Enterprises (TVEs) 62
Toyota Production System 16
transaction costs 50, 109–111, 124, 180
transcendent institutionalism 165, 167, 168
Transit 35
Truman, Harry 25
trust 3, 4, 24, 57, 102, 104, 105, 109, 111, 116, 121, 125, 137, 151, 153–155, 161, 163, 164, 180, 181, 188

United Airlines (UA) 82
United Nations 171

United States Air Force (USAF) 35, 36
US Army War College 45
US Cyber Command (USCYBERCOM) 38
University of Chicago 10
University of Pennsylvania 7
Unmanned Air Vehicle (UAV) *see* drones
Unmanned Combat Air Vehicle (UCAV) 36, 77

V1 34
V2 34
value-added re-seller 103
value-adding partnership 103
Value Based Management (VBM) 146
viral marketing 83
Virgin 21
Volker, Kurt 78
Voltaire 25, 26, 166
VUCA (Volatile, Uncertain, Complex, Ambiguous) *passim*

Waddington, C. H. 5
Wales, Jimmy 50
Waseda University 126
Washington Post 55
Watt, James 102
Welch, Jack 82
Wharton School of Finance and Commerce 7
White House 45, 97, 179
Wikipedia 50, 111
Williamson, Oliver 110
Willis, Bruce 40
winchester drive 92
Wollstonecraft, Mary 166
World Database of Happiness 171

xiao (filial piety) 66
Xiaogang farmers 62
Xinhua 68

Yahoo 46
yi (propriety) 66
Youtube 50, 52, 53, 82
Yuan Yafei 162
Yudkowsky, Eliezer 82
Zapatero, José Luis Rodríguez 51

zero-based budgeting (ZBB) xi, 140, 142–144, 148
zhong (loyalty) 66